BURN THE STAGE:

The Rise of BTS and Korean Boy Bands

BTS

NY Times Best-seller
MARC SHAPIRO

For more information contact:
Riverdale Avenue Books
5676 Riverdale Avenue
Riverdale, NY 10471.

www.riverdaleavebooks.com

Design by www.formatting4U.com
Cover by Scott Carpenter

Digital ISBN: 9781626014909

Print ISBN: 9781626014916

First Edition December, 2018

Dedication:

This book is dedicated to all of those who dare to dream, hope and believe. Hey you out there! If you want it bad enough, you can be anything you want to be and do anything you want to do. Don't take "no" for an answer.

Table of Contents

Author's Notes
The Next Big Thing

Pop culture has always been about the next big thing. Quite simply, it's the nature of the beast.

Talented creatives come out of nowhere, establish themselves in the public consciousness, creatively or otherwise, and then rise to whatever level of popularity or notoriety the fates have in store for them. The creatives then either flame out and disappear, or became grizzled veterans of stardom, destined for a decent run on the charts, the movies, on television screens or, yes, between the covers of best-selling books.

At the end of the day, it's all the luck of the draw, with a whole lot of talent, grit and determination thrown in for good measure. If you've got all those traits on your side and the gods are smiling, then you've got a shot

Those who have been around this cycle for any length of time swear up and down that the average life span of 'The Next Big Thing' is about three years. It's usually at that point that fans' minds wander, creative attitudes begin to change and real-life issues for come into play for both 'The Next Big Thing' and their audience. There are countless examples of performances of 'Here Today, Gone Tomorrow', especially in the checkered history of manufactured pop music where 'one hit wonders' are part of the landscape.

You've seen a lot of so-called manufactured superstars come and go in the 60's. Take Bobby Sherman for instance; a fairly low-profile actor making his way in Hollywood, but, after success in a short-run television series called *Here Comes The Brides*, the actor was suddenly the flavor of the moment and was shoe-horned into a pre-fab pop star career that served up a handful of semi-successful singles ("Julie Do You Love Me?" and "Easy Come, Easy Go") and a lot of touring over a three-year period. The intended audience quickly lost interest when *Here Comes the Brides* was cancelled and Sherman disappeared into the pop culture ether, living the later part of his life as a paramedic and a police officer.

The Partridge Family, a made-up band for a TV show, was somewhat cut from the same cloth, but the second life of the group was a bit more successful, as the show's actors were marginally talented musicians. *The Partridge Family* recorded hit albums and singles ("I Think I Love You") and would tour when the show of the same name was not in production. Once the show ran its course, the demise of *The Partridge Family* band followed shortly, with the exception of the show's most viable musician, David Cassidy, who would go on to mine a respectable career in the teeny bop recording and touring arenas.

Then there was *The Monkees,* a made-for-TV band partially modeled after the early Beatles. *The Monkees*, the real live off shoot of the fictional television series band, probably had the most success, thanks, in large part to the genius songwriting talents of Tommy Boyce and Bobby Hart. The band released a number of massive hit records during the life of the show and after ("Daydream Believer," "I'm a Believer," "Last Train to Clarksville" and "Pleasant Valley Sunday*")*. Likewise, the cycle ended with the cancellation of the TV series, but their catchy pop tunes have survived the decades on classic rock radio and occasional concerts by the surviving members.

The history lesson is over. But as you can see, there has always been a method to this madness, especially when it comes to enterprising producers and business types who are quite happy to capitalize on the always mercurial teen market.

Bottom line, pop idols are born, live and die on the wings of fate, timing and a whole lot of elements in the universe that they cannot truly control. Many are around so fleetingly that journalists, authors and chroniclers usually don't get on board 'The Next Big Thing' before it's already time to get onto the next big thing waiting in the wings. Timing is everything in this business. None of this is meant to denigrate the system. It's not good or bad. It's just the way things work when you're attempting to catch lightning in a bottle.

Which is why I was glad to get the opportunity to follow the odyssey of Korean K-Pop stars BTS early on their rise with *Burn the Stage: The Rise of BTS and Korean Boy Bands*. This feisty group of South Korean pop stars were born of an age-old music adage; take complete unknowns, mold them, shape them, polish them and out pops performers totally into performing in a niche that needs to be filled.

The target audience is, more often than not, young teenage girls, the vehicle easy to digest, songs with simple lyrics and direct messages, all set to an easy-to-follow instrumental beat. The messengers, cute, charismatic young boys who tug at the heartstrings and the fantasies of girls dreaming of first boyfriends and first love that is driven by the fan magazines (and, in this case, the Internet) and the willingness to say yes to everything in the name of pop music stardom. Something that the members of BTS seem to have in spades. Make no mistake, being pop music idols is hard work and it has helped that the members of BTS have been more than willing to take the ride.

The history of BTS is being measured in years, but not many at this point. The three-year cycle is coming to a head, but what makes BTS (aka *The Bangtan Boys*) something different? Their career at this point has been more measured and, by degrees, less frantic. Their rise to pop stardom has been a gradual ascension. First, South Korea, then Asia, then Europe and finally, in 2018, the group is shouldering their way into the United States on the strength of their hit records and seemingly non-stop touring.

So, I saw this as a chance to follow the bouncing ball and to show exactly what goes into making a modern-day pop group, how BTS found their way to stardom and how the band was born. In a way this is like *American Idol* and, in a way, it's a sterling example of how creativity and business can join forces to spit out something new, exciting and, as future historians will debate, a legitimate by-product of the times.

I know there are probably cynics out there who would roll their eyes at the prospect of anybody spending a lot of hours on something that would appear so trivial. To those I would say, you're missing the boat. BTS and all it encompasses is an important milestone in a person's life, be they young or old. It ignites the passion and potential in an often stagnant world and brings smiles and a sense of hope and happiness. If we're being honest, we've all experienced such moments. A favorite band. A first kiss or relationship. Emotionally and psychologically, we've all had moments that have put us fully in the driver's seat of life.

Actual research into this group would be a challenge. The vast majority of coverage of *BTS*, especially in their formative years, was generated overseas and, largely, in Korea and in the Korean language. But thanks to my computer's trusty translation device, I was able to pull much of the band's earliest memories and anecdotes into the English-speaking world. This being a teen band, there was also the matter of the journalism surrounding BTS being largely on a *Tiger Beat* and *Teen Vogue* level, lots of "what is your favorite color?" and "what do you look for in a girl?" inquiries. But all the inherent puffery aside, the members of *BTS* were nothing if not serious about their lives and career and it would show with regularity in deep insights and anecdotes. While the members of *BTS* have been well-rehearsed, they've also been allowed the freedom to speak their minds.

And it was with a bit more mature attitude in mind that I hoped to raise the bar a few notches. There is plenty of material for fans, the bits and pieces of the pop star life, the things that most people would think are ultimately inconsequential but to diehard fans are the Holy Grail of knowledge. But lurking in the shadows of BTS and K-Pop is a well-defined history and business acumen that are equally enlightening (some possibly less than glamorous things that ultimately make a BTS possible). Look out for those moments and savor them as well.

Will the readers of *Burn the Stage: The Rise of BTS and Korean Boy Bands* get it? I believe so, because part of being hip and cool is also about being observant, curious and everything that goes along with figuring out life, be it pop stars or equally important things about the future.

K-Pop, the style of music that has spawned BTS, has been around a while and this book covers its history. This book also has the personal and professional insights into individuals who have come together to make the BTS whole. Creating a BTS in the modern world had its own set of challenges and hurdles and, you will glimpse how that works.

At the end of the day, *Burn the Stage: The Rise of BTS and Korean Boy Bands* is, finally, pop culture of 2018 observed through a lens of change, and, in the hearts of the very young, the souls of hopes, dreams and fantasies. Welcome to 'The Next Big Thing.' Long may it reign.

Marc Shapiro
2018

Introduction
Too Cool

Downtown Los Angeles can be like a ghost town in the morning.

The expected traffic snarl of people driving to work has not yet reached its peak, with only a smattering of car noises echoing through the concrete jungle of high-rise buildings that reach, literally, to the sky. Trash trucks on their early appointed rounds and store owners pulling back iron grates and opening their shops pass for activity in the early morning hours as the sun begins its ascent through the overcast. All is calm in downtown Los Angeles on September 5, 2018.

Everywhere except the Staples Center, where the BTS "Army"— the name given to the fanatic followers of the South Korean pop stars— is out in full force as they await the first show and the official unveiling of the first BTS US tour. This is not the first time that fans have lined up for hours before a show they just had to see. We've all seen the videos enraptured fans of Elvis, The Beatles, Justin Bieber and an endless number of entertainers who had played live in the 'City of Angels.' But this being BTS, the vibe was decidedly different.

One could sense an aura of excitement, exuberance and a rush of youthful expectation as the crowd snaked

1

out from the Staples Center, down Pico Boulevard and around the LA Live entertainment complex, easily numbering in the thousands. Those standing in line were primarily young teen girls, an ethnically diverse group, whose expectations and dreams of seeing a live concert by their emotional and musical crushes were about to be fulfilled. And they had pulled out all the stops to make their dreams come true.

As television reporters swooped in, cameras and microphones at the ready to capture the excitement, they were greeted with screams of enthusiasm and the occasional tears as those lined up to tell the lengths they had gone through to get in line early and to get the coveted tickets. One girl proudly exclaimed that she had been camping outside the Staples Center for more than 24 hours to secure a place at the front of the line. Another said she had quit her job in order to see all of the Los Angeles shows. The group's Los Angeles shows had long since sold out but the rumor along the line was that the first 100 people in line would receive a wristband that would gain the concert goers access to a special 'pit' area in front of the stage and in close proximity to the group. That was all the young teens needed to hear.

One girl, jumping up and down in anticipation and excitement, told a television news reporter, "I'm so nervous and excited at the same time! I can't wait to see them! I'm hoping I can be so close to them!"

The doors to the Staples Center concert arena would be opening in two and a half hours. Thousands of teenagers could hardly wait. The first date of a month-long US tour would begin shortly and end, thousands of miles and many months later on October 6, 2018 in a massive New York baseball stadium, much like The

Beatles did some decades earlier. For *BTS*, the tour was significant. It was the beginning of a long march and the final step in completing world domination.

The five-year reign of BTS (whose members are RM, J-Hope, Suga, Jin, Jimin, V and Jungkook) in other parts of the world had finally found its way to the United States in 2017 when an extensive publicity and media blitz, coupled with the band members beginning to work with more established music stars like The Chainsmokers and Steve Aoki, finally resulted in America's early acceptance of BTS*'s* music.

The first indication that BTS was making inroads into America's music consciousness came in September, 2017 when their album *Love Yourself: Her* became the first Korean language album to enter the *Billboard 200* album chart. Around that time, the group's single "DNA" would join the march on US sensibilities when it reached No. 67 on the *Billboard Hot 100* singles charts, the highest position on that chart for a K-Pop group. By December 2017, a second BTS single, "Mic Drop", would debut on the *Billboard Hot 100* chart at No. 28.

In May, 2018, BTS would make history when their album *Love Yourself: Tear* would top the *Billboard* album chart. By September, the group would duplicate that feat when their next album, *Love Yourself: Answer* would also capture the top spot on the *Billboard* album chart.

And one thing had become certain in the years leading up to the conquest of America. The members of BTS were not stereotypical pop stars, literal puppets on a corporate string. They had grown to become quite savvy in the business side of what they were doing. A trait typified by an interview band member RM did with the

3

all-business all the time *Forbes Magazine* in which he reflected on the importance of their US breakthrough with the album *Love Yourself: Her*.

"I think we're always doing something for teenagers and youngsters," he said. "BTS originally performed itself as a socially conscious band. We always wanted to sell our performances. I think what makes this album really special is that it is a real turning point for us. It has a new concept, to love yourself, and I think fans are really reacting to it. The music is trendier. So I think our history, the music and the new concept has maxed this time. Everything was perfect so the *Billboard* thing could happen."

But RM acknowledged that BTS, in their wildest imagination, could not have predicted the success the group was having in America. "It's still like we're dreaming. *The Billboard 200 Top Ten* is not something that I thought we could achieve. I feel like we are so lucky and so grateful to the fans."

The sold-out crowd at the Staples Center was boiling over with anticipation. Opening nights of a lengthy tour are like that, for the audience and performers alike. For most of those in the audience this was their first chance to witness BTS live. Whatever the big reveal would be, the adrenaline was surging at whatever was about to take place.

Suddenly there was a flickering of lights, a loud wash of music and the members of BTS raced onto the stage. Screams beyond mere decibels erupted and echoed around the cavernous arena. The BTS Army was on the march and their generals were ready for action.

The choreography was flawless, a polished well-rehearsed counterpoint to the vocal harmonies that ran staccato lines of emotion around each song. From the first song, there was something musically for every taste, swinging rhythm & blues mixed and meshed into waves of spirited club music, pile-driving pop and hip hop and more than a smattering of emo. The ballads were pure, thoughtful and direct in extolling the virtues of independence and freedom that captured those young at heart and innocent in nature. The hip hop songs came across as a restrained heathenism, with messages that were daring yet not crossing any pre-conceived line.

Even those who may well have seen it all before, the polished stance of boy bands past, present and future, a bit of 'N'Sync, a touch of The Jonas Bros and the implied innocence and naughty nature of The Jackson 5, had to admit that there was something quite different going on this night. This was a presentation that defied preconceived notions. The group's style and the way they presented themselves and their songs was something exciting and new.

The theatrics of it all, which saw the group switching in and out of costumes, everything from black and gold matador costumes, frilly white blouses and baggy tracksuits, were seemingly of the moment, seemingly spontaneous and appropriate to the songs. This was a concert dialed in to a generation raised on technology, social media and the concept of immediate, spontaneous gratification. And for them, BTS had gotten it right.

At one point in the show, the members of BTS, seemingly overcome with emotion of the moment, stood at stage center, smiling as the crowd roaring out their adulation, grateful for the experience.

And so was BTS.

Chapter One
Before There Was BTS

History shows that BTS is only the latest incarnation of K-Pop. How far back one wants to go back to the true roots of the Korean form depends on how hard one wants to work. Some point to the song "Gangnam Style" as a jumping off point for the emergence of K-Pop as a modern at-large fixture in the international pop music world. But to get to the true beginnings of the genre, and diligent researchers from *Billboard*, *A Side.com* and *Vox.com* have done just that, one must travel back much further.

To 1885.

When missionary Henry Appenzeller began to broaden the world view of Korean children by teaching American and British folk songs, replacing the original English lyrics with Korean lyrics. Appenzeller's musical experiment came at a very tense political time. Beginning with Japan's takeover of Korea in 1910, and lasting until the end of Japan's rule in 1945, those early songs, known quite simply as *Changga,* were banned by the Japanese on the grounds that many of the song's lyrics expressed anti-Japanese sentiments.

Nineteen forty-five brought an end of conflict in Korea when Japan was driven from Korea and, in the wake of the Korean War, Western and Korean culture began to mix and mingle. One of the most pivotal moments would turn out to be *Trot* music, a Korean version of American popular music whose influences drew heavily on the *Changga* lexicon. *Trot* would be considered by many historians to be the very first form of Korean pop music.

The Kim Sisters, a trio consisting of Sook-ja, Aija and Minja, would pioneer K-Pop in 1959, when after a number of years playing a mixture of country and rock music for US troops, they left Korea for America where they became a popular draw at *The Stardust Hotel* in Las Vegas. In the audience for one of their Las Vegas shows was television variety show host Ed Sullivan, who invited *The Kim Sisters* to perform for what would be the first of 20 appearances on his top rated *The Ed Sullivan Show*, thus bringing the earliest form of K-Pop to an American audience.

Throughout the decade of the 60's, the ever-evolving K-Pop genre, honed primarily by Korean musicians who would play for and be influenced by US troops, would regularly run afoul of Korean political intrigue throughout the 60's and early 70's. *Add 4*, featuring the distinctive rock and roll stylings of guitarist Shin Jung-hyeon, had the distinction of being the first rock and roll band to appear in Korea. All went well until Korean President Park Chung-hee requested that Shin compose a song in his honor. When Shin refused the request, Park brought the full wrath of his militaristic government to bear on the musician. He had Shin arrested on questionable drug charges and sentenced him to two years in prison. After his release, *Add 4* was banned from performing.

7

Around the time Shin was in prison, another Korean emerged who would rub the government the wrong way. Singer-songwriter Han Dae-soo, born in Korea but who spent his childhood in America, returned to Korea and established himself as a folk singer of much renown, much in the tradition of John Lennon and Bob Dylan. Two well received albums, *Long Long Road* and *Rubber Shoes* are considered seminal contributions to K-Pop lore. But when the aforementioned President Park felt that many of Soo's songs contained anti-government messages, the singer was forced to leave Korea and return to the states.

Billed as the Korean version of Michael Jackson, Cho Yong-pil was yet another performer who cut his teeth on entertaining US troops. Cho would find true success in 1975 with his first single "Come Back to Busan Port." Cho, who would find the majority of his popularity in Korea and Japan, would parlay his success into two memorable concert appearances, becoming the first Korean singer to perform in Carnegie Hall and one of only a handful of South Korean performers to perform in North Korea.

By the 1980's, K-Pop was entering a new phase. Gone to a large extent were the rock and more progressive forms of music and in their place was a new generation of ballad singers whose commercial, predictable and often schmaltzy odes to love and romance became the rage throughout South Korea. One of the most popular performers to emerge from the ballad singer period, Gwang-jo Lee, would sell an estimated 300,000 copies of his album *You're Too Far Away to Get Close To*.

The ballad singer years would make an evolutionary turn in the 90's to a style that was very much the forerunner of BTS. For South Korea, this would be the decade of "The Boy Bands" and a more modern, beat-oriented brand of pop. Ground zero for the new style of K-Pop would be *Seo Taiji & Boys*, with their hip-hop and swing influences being 'the next big thing' for their time and their success would literally open the floodgates for this next generation. HOT (*High-five of Teenagers*) were quick to jump on the bandwagon of Korean boy bands and would become the first Korean pop group to sell a million albums.

HOT's record label, SM Entertainment, knew an exploitable trend when they saw it and were quick to capitalize when, through a rigorous audition and pop star boot camp process, they created an all-female counter to HOT called SES. SES would equal and then surpass the success of HOT. By the year 2000, K-Pop had become a cash cow of enormous proportion, one that was acknowledged as an industry that was keeping an up and down South Korean economy afloat. It was a creative venture that made millions of music lovers happy.

And as it turned out, was ripe with abuse.

The major K-Pop record labels had morphed into, essentially, artist management and image consulting firms. They created the groups and maintained legal control over their creations. The typical K-Pop contract was extremely long running and weighted heavily toward absolute control by the labels. Very little of the money made through record sales, touring and merchandizing was actually going to the groups.

Complaints were mounting and legal investigation of the K-Pop contract practices became commonplace. Finally, the Korean Fair Trade Commission stepped in to attempt to save this black eye on the face of the Korean economy, creating what was termed a 'model contract' for labels and artists and a government-supported organization where K-Pop artists could seek legal advice. It was considered a small contribution to artists' rights as the concept of creating manufactured pop culture would continue well into the 2000's.

By 2006, yet another record company creation, Big Bang, became the high-water mark for the boy band industry. During their lifetime, Big Bang would sell more than 140,000,000 records, spin its group members off into equally successful solo careers and, by 2015, would be dubbed 'the biggest boy band in the world' by *The Hollywood Reporter*. Following the equally successful path of manufactured/reality show creations were the groups Girl's Generation and Twice, both groups that followed the path to stardom that seemed to run between Korea and Japan.

It would remain for 2012's "Gangnam Style" by Psi, a poppy bit of K-Pop dance music, to finally kick open the K-Pop genre on a fully international scale that would include America. "Gangnam Style" benefitted from a pop culture-friendly Psi who had invented the now famous "horse dance" for an accompanying video that, to date, has collected more than 2.8 billion views.

The history of K-Pop is ongoing and ever-evolving. New acts seemingly poised for stardom are announced along the K-Pop pipeline on a weekly basis, spreading the divergent sounds on a worldwide axis. The latest chapter in that history is now unveiling in real time.

It is BTS. And they are on the move.

Chapter Two
Meet The Boys:

RM

RM (real name Kim Nam-joon) was born on September 12, 1994 in Islan Gygeonngi- South Korea. He was educated in *Apaujeong High School* and *Global Cyber University*. He would spend six months studying and living in New Zealand. Although he was proceeding on a course of an engineering major, early on he became attracted to pop music, particularly rap and hip hop. RM was influenced by US rappers such as Nas and Eminem and the likes of K-Pop stalwart *Epik High*. His first attempts at writing rap lyrics would be immortalized on scraps of paper that he hid in his sixth grade school books, lest his interest in rap be discovered by those who might disapprove. The older he got, the more inclined RM was to follow his rap dreams.

"I loved writing lyrics for rap when I was in junior high school," he revealed to *Elle*. "I knew at that point that, somehow, I wanted to be a rapper who can write and rap."

Consequently, the notion of a formal education and a more traditional future began to lose its appeal.

"I used to study hard," he told *Cuvism Magazine*.

11

"But when I studied, I had no dreams. There was nothing I wanted to do with what I was learning."

Thanks to the insistence of his parents, RM was, by his teenage years, already learning to speak English by watching endless hours of television news programs on the *BBC* and *CNN*. It is rather unorthodox approach to mastering the English language that he jokingly discussed during an appearance on *The Ellen DeGeneres Show*. "My English teacher watched the television sitcom *Friends*. Back in the days, when I was 14, 15, it was like a syndrome for all the Korean parents to make their kids watch *Friends*. I thought I was kind of like a victim at that time but, right now, I consider myself the lucky one. Thanks to my mother who bought all the seasons of *Friends* on DVD."

During his teen years, RM would cautiously enter the rap scene, becoming a minor sensation on the Korean underground rap circuit. He performed regularly in the trendy rap center of *Hongdae*, occasionally performing under the stage name of Runch Randa and as part of his very first rap crew called DNH which saw the youngster going head to head with other upcoming talents including Iron, Supreme Boi and Kidoh.

He would occasionally cross paths with an equally promising young performer named J-Hope whose dance moves proved a compliment to RM's emerging lyrical and vocal talents. Having performed live with rapper Zico and as part of the *Crew of the South Korean Hip Hop Cooperative*, and having recorded some very early raps with producer Bang who, according to RM in a *Time Magazine* interview, was immediately encouraging. "I was an underground rapper and only 16 years old.

Bang thought I had potential as a rapper and a lyricist. And so we went from there."

It was at that point that an engineering career lost out to rap and RM began toying with the idea of forming a serious group.

J-Hope

J-Hope (real name Jung Ho-seok) was born on February 18, 1994 in Gwangju, South Korea. From a very early age, J-Hope seemed born to perform. "When I was a little kid, I simply loved music and enjoyed expressing myself with my body," he told *Elle*. "Everyone liked me when I went up onstage at a talent search in elementary school and that's when I decided to become a music artist."

J-Hope was further inspired during his middle school years after watching videos of foreign dancers and decided he would become a professional dancer. His drive and desire would carry him through his high school years and into his first brush with public notoriety as part of the underground street dance team called Neuron.

J-Hope remembered those days in conversation with *Cuvism*. "While promoting underground with my street dance team, I did a lot of Popping. In Popping there was another subgenre called Boogaloos and that was the one I did a lot. I got a lot of prizes and performed a lot."

Encouraged by his early success, J-Hope took an important step forward when he auditioned for JYP Entertainment but did not make it to the final round. The youngster was disappointed but not discouraged.

He continued to attend talent agency auditions and eventually struck gold with Big Hit Entertainment and was accepted for the company's training program.

J-Hope quickly adjusted to the company's stringent yet encouraging program and took every opportunity to expand his horizons. Among his credits during his training days was as a backup dancer for the group GLAM*'s* video for the song "Glamorous." He worked with Jo Kwon as a featured rapper on the songs "Animal" and "I'm Da One."

Jimin

Jimin (real name Park Ji-min) was born on October 13, 1995 in Busan, South Korea. Like any child, Jimin's early childhood memories were populated by dreams that led to his family being bombarded with what their son hoped to be when he grew up. "I had many dreams as a child that were inspired by cartoons," he told *BTS Live*. "I wanted to be a scientist, a police officer, a race car driver, a martial artist and a swordsman."

By age two, Jimin was also showing an interest in dancing and would go on to spend his early childhood years balancing formal education with an after-school dance program. "I was serious about it," he said. "I wanted to learn dancing properly."

Jimin remembered those days in an interview with *BTS Japan Fan Magazine*. "I became interested in dancing at an early age and entered dance academy. Whenever I had time, I would go and practice dance. I participated in big performances but I was really nervous in those days."

A big part of Jimin's life was consumed with

financial concerns. His family was not wealthy and when he became concerned about the high cost of tuition fees, he considered dropping out of the dance academy. "However, my dance academy teacher said I could attend even if I didn't pay. That teacher took so much care of me and I wanted to repay the teacher so I practiced even harder."

Jimin's dancing aspirations turned serious in the eighth grade after watching a stirring performance by the dance group Rain. He would follow this dream for a number of years, matriculating between the Busan High School of The Arts and Korea Arts High School, majoring in modern dance. But while dance was his passion, it would soon be joined by another artistic dream.

"In the ninth grade, I decided that I wanted to become a singer," he explained to *BTS Live*. "I have to be one. Being a singer means I can be loved a lot, more than anyone could be easily loved."

But it would be his dance skills, along with the insistence of a Department of Dance teacher from his School of the Arts days that finally convinced Jimin to audition for *Big Hit Entertainment*. After being accepted, he moved to Seoul and Big Hit's training program where his natural skills soon came to the agencies' notice during back dancing assignments for GLAM's live performances and videos. In short order, Jimin would be ready for the big time.

Suga

Suga (real name Min Yoon-gi) was born on March 9, 1993 in Dageu, South Korea. Suga told *Japanese BTS*

Fan Magazine that his early childhood was marked by a restless streak. "When I was young, I was pretty much an ordinary kid. I loved playing around so my kindergarten teacher didn't seem to like me. I remember being scolded a lot."

In the same interview, Suga related that he was quite mature in many ways as a youngster. "I had a thing for collecting. I collected a lot of books when I was young. It was a time when I wanted to be a cultured man. I wanted to pretend that I knew things."

Suga was attracted to all kinds of music at a fairly early age, specifically hip hop and rap and, in particular the music of Stony Skunks and Epik High. By age 12, Suga had discovered his life path.

Within a year, Suga had taken that important next step. "When I was 13, I began writing my own lyrics," he told *Grazia Korea*. When Suga turned 17, he landed a part time job at a recording studio where he received on-the-job training in the music business, composing, arranging and making and selling beats.

Equally important, Suga was coming to terms with his own creative skills in rapping and performing and was taking his act to the public in the ever-widening underground rap community. "I went on stage for the first time during my second year in middle school at a festival. I remember I performed Dynamic Duo's song 'Go Back.' I didn't like standing in front of people at that point but I felt I had to do it."

Suga, performing under the name of "Gloss" as part of an up and coming hip hop crew called D-Town, began to make an impression, first by way of an appearance in the music video of J Kwon's song "In The One" and releasing his first song under the D

Town banner entitled "518-062." His growing notoriety led to Suga producing music for other rappers, one of the better known credits of that day being the Reflow song "Who Am I?"

Suga was ready for the next big step in his musical odyssey. He would not have to wait long.

He had seen a flyer advertising a Big Hit Entertainment rap/talent audition and had decided it would be a good step forward career-wise, not necessarily as a performer but as a chance to further his producing credits. Suga came in second place in the audition and was subsequently signed to Big Hit as a trainee. Although he was not completely sold on the idea of being a performer, his time as a trainee would result in some performing assignments, as a dancer in the group GLAM's live performance of the song "Glamorous," the live performances of the hologram artist SeeU and as a backup dancer in a sequence of the Jo Kwon video "I'm Da One."

V

V (real name Kim Tae-hyung) was born on December 30, 1995 in Daegu, South Korea. V's family were farmers and the way he often described it, if all else failed he would be welcomed back to the family business. But by the time he reached high school, V was already destined for something different.

"I have always been a bright kid since kindergarten days so my teachers adored me a lot," he told the *BTS Japan Official Fan Magazine*. "In elementary school I was a bright kid who wanted to know a lot. I didn't imagine doing anything except farm jobs in the future but I still thought I had to study hard. That all changed after I fell in love with music."

After viewing videos from international musician Danny Fung, V was inspired to take up the saxophone. Encouraged by his family, the youngster was inspired and would spend the next few years in serious study with the instrument. But with time, V's interests began to wander and by the time he entered Korean Arts High School, he was on to something different. "I suddenly got interested in dancing and decided to take a different path. I wanted to focus on dancing. Even if I became a singer, I wouldn't be cool if I couldn't dance."

One day, V went with a friend to a Big Hit Entertainment audition. He had not been interested in auditioning himself but, simply, to go and support his friend. But during the course of just hanging out, someone from the talent agency spotted V and urged him to audition. In a matter of moments, V was on the telephone with his father who gave him the okay to go ahead. V auditioned and, as it would turn out, would be the only contestant to pass the audition that day.

Big Hit Entertainment immediately knew they had found a diamond in the rough but decided to keep his presence with the company secret until they had devised a definite plan for him. Except for a fleeting moment as a bodyguard in Jo Kwon's video for the song "I'm Da O," V would remain a deep, dark secret.

Jungkook

Jungkook (real name Jeon Jung-kook) was born on September 1, 1997 in Busan, South Korea. At an early age Jungkook adopted a very mature philosophy on life. "I would rather be dead than to live without passion," he offered to *Fandom.com*. And what Jungkook was passionate about in his early years was sports, especially badminton, which he dreamed of becoming a professional player. His youthful sports ambitions would guide him through years as a student at Baek Middle School and, later the Seoul School of the Performing Arts.

But his interest would change in his pre-teen years as he gravitated toward all things pop culture and especially music. It was at age 11 that Jungkook would make a decisive decision when he became a devotee of the Korean pop/hip hop/ rap music scene. Two songs in particular would guide him, IU's "Lost Child" and G Dragon's "Heartbreaker." *G Dragon* was impressive," Jungkook told *Ize Magazine*, "and I decided that I wanted to be just like him."

But as he explained in *Ize,* he was not in any hurry. "When I was younger, I thought that everything would just come to me eventually."

Jungkook continued to explore the music, hanging out with friends at all ages clubs and watching and learning what went into song stylings and performance. He was a quick study and his talents soon made him the talk of the town. He eventually mustered up the courage, at age 12, to audition for the popular Superstar K talent show which had long been the proving grounds for talents who would be plucked from obscurity and into the spotlight.

Jungkook attended the audition and, according to observers, did quite well in the preliminary rounds but was ultimately eliminated before the final rounds of the competition. But those in the industry liked a lot of what they saw and, shortly after the competition, a total of seven record and entertainment talent agencies were actively scouting Jungkook with an eye toward getting him into their training programs.

Jungkook was flattered at the attention. And when the dust settled, there would be one offer that he could not refuse. He had come to know RM and had been overwhelmed with his rapping and performing skills. The opportunity to be in the same company and to train with him made Jungkook's decision easy.

He would sign with Big Hit Entertainment.

Jin

Jin (real name Kim Seok -jin) was born on December 4, 1992 in Anyang City in the Gaucheon, South Korea province. His first memories began at age two when his family moved to Gaucheon City. And as he recalled in an interview with the *Japanese Official BTS Fan Magazine*, a big part of those early years he was quite camera shy. "I was awkward about taking photos for a long time so I hardly have any childhood photos. It's hard to find photos of me from back then. When you take photos you have to stand still. I hated hearing 'Wait, let's just take one photo!' and having to stand still."

A bright, sensitive and inquisitive child. An older brother introduced Jin to much of Korean pop culture and, particularly, hip hop music. However, it would be more of a childhood attraction than an avocation.

By the time Jin reached high school, Jin was leaning toward fairly traditional occupations. "In the first year of high school my dream was to become a newspaper reporter to stand by the second class citizen's side," he told the *Japanese Fan Magazine*. "I used to read newspaper articles everyday

At certain points in his life, his outlook for his future was more traditional. "I might have turned out to be a farmer," he said in a *CNBC* article, "because I used to do farming when I was in middle school." Although he was enticed by the prospect of music in his life, he was equally and more seriously drawn to the theatrics of acting. "The dream of becoming an actor was born in my second year of high school after watching the drama *Queen Seondeok*. I was touched and thought that I wanted to make people cry with my acting."

His interest would flourish during his years in Konkuk University as an acting major and it began to look more and more that Jin's future and fame would center on the performing stage.

As was the custom of the time, scouts for various talent agencies were quite literally on the streets, looking for potential clients. Jin's quite striking and exotic looks made him a possible target for talent scouts and, on a particular day, a scout for a well-known agency approached Jin as he was walking down the street and offered to sign him to a contract. Jin was leery of the sincerity and, yes, honesty of the talent scout's pitch and rejected the offer.

Yet another approach would come his way that seemed sincere and promising; Jin was spotted exiting a bus when he was approached by a representative of Big Hit Entertainment. The agency wanted to sign him but wanted to know if he could sing and dance. Jin's response was that he could not do either and had no idea about where to begin. But the agency was convinced that Jin had that certain something they were looking for.

And as to the singing and dancing? They were confident that he could learn.

But in the meantime, Jin was given every opportunity to act in Big Hit Entertainment productions such as the Jo Kwon video for the song "I'm Da One" in which he played the role of a bodyguard and butler. But it would be his dedication to hard work and hours of practice that would ultimately make him boy band ready.

Chapter Three
Making the Band

Bang Si-hyuk had been around the music industry long enough to have seen it all. As a teen he cut his early creative teeth in the heavy metal world. His ambitions to make a living in music had instantly put him at odds with his family. But even his parents had to admit that, when it came to the fine art of creating music, he was quite good.

As a founding member of the JYP Talent Agency in the mid 90's, Bang proved a natural when it came to crafting K-Pop songs. He was proficient and extremely commercial, creating and arranging such as the God's "One Candle," T-ara's "Like the First Time" and countless pop hits by the likes of Wonder Girls, Rain and Teen Top, thus earning the respectful industry nickname of Hit Man.

Bang was an introspective, free thinking sort which, by turns, made him uneasy at the monopoly of talent agencies that, through the implementation of extremely toxic, controlling contracts, had succeeded in squeezing the creative life out of numerous K-Pop groups. In many cases, they were kept virtual prisoners in a cycle of touring and recording and turning legitimate creative talents into glorified robots who were forcefully programmed to conform to a corporate line.

Personal lives were considered taboo by what were considered "slave contracts" that the agencies held over the heads of budding idol groups and superstars alike. Being caught dating or taking drugs was considered a betrayal of image and their fans and could result in hospitalization or dismissal from the group. Bang saw examples of this prison-like approach to making pop culture entertainment on a near daily basis and it disturbed him.

Bang was also a restless spirit who found the high degree of conformity and predictability that chaffed his sense of individuality and freedom. And although he was a founding member of the company, he was finding himself being bossed around by people he considered his equals in the company.

Which was why, in 2005, he left JYP to start his own company, Big Hit Entertainment. He was intent on creating a new kind of K-Pop. But there would be bumps in the road. The handful of early clients on the Big Hit Entertainment roster were not delivering the kind of success Bang had become accustomed to. The 2009 regional hit "Without a Heart" was the company's first regional hit. At one point, Big Hit Entertainment was teetering close to bankruptcy. It was at that point that Bang decided to put together his notions for a boy band.

In his mind, Bang had a blueprint for what would be an anti-establishment (by Korean cultural standards) and anti-K-Pop rules. His dream group would write their own songs and lyrics. Their lyrics would be socially conscious, in keeping with the real world hopes and dreams of their fans. They would create and manage their own media presence rather than conform to manufactured personas. Entire albums rather than individual singles would be the marketing approach. Group members would be free to talk about the struggles and pressures of their lives and careers. And, perhaps most importantly to Bang's way of thinking, he would do away with the concept of "slave contracts" and grueling schedules.

Bang came down firmly on the side of creativity in a conversation with *X Ports News.com* when he offered, "My hope is that they would become a group that could write and perform their own performances." He would be philosophical in a *SOOMPI.com* interview when he stated, "I didn't want them to be false idols. I wanted to create a group that could become a close friend."

Always considered a deep thinker in a pop culture industry that was characterized by imitating what was popular at the moment, Bang would think long and hard about his grand plan for this new kind of K-Pop. And he would wax philosophical and profound when it came to something as simple as picking a group name. It began with a Korean expression, "Bangtan Sonyeondan" which translated into the term Bulletproof Boy Scouts or, in its embryonic stage BTS. In an *Affinity.com* article, BTS member J-Hope gave a succinct accounting of what it all meant. "It [the name] has a profound meaning. Bangtan means to be resistant to bullets, so it means to block out stereotypes, criticisms and expectations that aim at adolescents, like bullets, to preserve the values and ideals of today's adolescents."

During the evolution of the group, Bang would, perhaps in the name of commercial attitudes, lean heavily on BTS as meaning Beyond The Scene, acknowledging the group's intended audience as a generation in evolution who were moving beyond the realities they were facing and heading into a future of new possibilities.

But before he could implement his grand plans, Bang needed a musical hook to hang his hopes and dreams on. Which led him to look at his young trainee RM for direction. The pair had crossed paths when RM had auditioned for a hip-hop crew. Through the audition he met rap and hip hop impresario Sleepy who was so impressed with RM's skills that he passed RM's phone number onto Bang who was equally impressed and signed him to a trainee contract with Big Hit with an eye toward turning the young boy into a solo rap artist. He had not been in the training program very long when Bang, in 2010, decided that his early incarnation of BTS would be an all hip-hop/rap group.

On initial take, that version of BTS was formidable, teaming RM with a group of equally talented rappers Kidoh, Iron, Supreme Boi, and, last but not least, Suga. But after a relatively short period of preparation, Bang, unexpectedly, took a creative right turn with his project and BTS suddenly turned from a crew of tough rappers to what appeared to be yet another idol style boy band.

Bang's change of mind would be questioned by many observers of the K-Pop scene. But to Bang, in a *CelebMix.com* story, it all seemed to make sense. "After seeing RM rap, I thought about creating a hip-hop group. Later I thought that the group just shouldn't be idols.

26

Chapter Four
Almost a Bangtan Boy

Word spread fast after it was announced that Bang Si-hyuk's new super group was now recruiting trainees. Bang's reputation in the K-Pop industry and the speculation that The Bangtan Boys would offer up something new to the tried and true K-Pop elements led to both newcomers and veterans lining up to take a shot at stardom.

But this being K-Pop, there were certain requirements of the genre that would give some applicants pause. The type of music would give some veterans or those musically ambitious reason to say thanks but no thanks. Then there was the matter of age. Perceived as teen acts for teen audiences, K-Pop groups were age conscious. Turning 20 was considered old in the boy band industry and even those on the low side of that figure were tentative about what their longevity might be. Of course, there was the upside. Stardom and more money than the budding BTS/ Bangtan Boys could ever imagine.

And so they came and, along the way, many quite good performers would wash out or call it a day and go home. Among the more notable casualties of those early BTS auditions and training periods were, as reported by *Pop Asia.com*…

i11even had already garnered quite the reputation on the underground rap circuit as a member of the DNH crew. To many of his followers, training to be a member of a boy band seemed a creative come on. But i11even would take a shot and would last through a fairly long training period before the stress and strain of adjusting to a boy band lifestyle proved too much and he left the program.

Beenzino had also emerged from the underground rap community with an attitude that seemed to make him a long shot for BTS. But as the training progressed, he emerged as a frontrunner who, at one point, was offered a position in the group. But for reasons unknown to this point, Beenzino chose to turn the opportunity down.

Loco was part of the new wave of potential boy band types who had emerged on the scene and was considered a potentially solid choice during the early stages of the audition process. But Loco would not last long and would be cut early in the auditions.

Basick was big on style and attitude and was another seemingly natural choice during the training days and was, at one point, offered a slot in what would be the initial incarnation of *BTS*. But like Beenzino he would say thanks but no thanks.

Reddy was another relative newcomer who showed promise but, after a highly competitive round of auditions, would come up short and would be cut.

Iron looked to be a solid entry into the first incarnation of *BTS*. But, aesthetically, he had a problem with the prefab nature of the process and the often prison-like observation and isolation associated with the training program before leaving. Supreme Boi was actually one of the founding members of the early BTS concept but, like Iron, chaffed at the constrictive nature of the process and left. But he would go on to become an important element of the BTS universe as a producer and writer on many of the group's albums.

Kidoh was yet another former member of the DNH rap crew whose personality and talent when it came to hip-hop kept him in the running for almost a year before he balked at the Spartan existence that went into becoming a boy band member and left the program. Styles would seem to be a stumbling block to making the BTS lineup for many during the audition stage. A-Tom and Suwoong being two cases in point. The former would wash out fairly early in the training regime but would go on to find success with the groups JBJ and Xeno-T while the later would leave the BTS boot camp but would find a measure of success two years later with the group Boy's Republic.

There would be countless stories like these as the auditions and training camp evolved. One thing was certain. Just as somebody left the program, there would be another entering with the dreams of stardom on their mind.

Chapter Five
Training Days

By 2010, the odyssey of BTS had begun in earnest.

The earliest concept for BTS was that the group would be a duo, consisting of RM and Iron. But it would not take long for Bang to reconfigure the concept as a group. During that first year, i11even, Suga and J-Hope were also cast and fast-tracked to be part of BTS. The following year, 2011, saw the rappers Kidoh and Supreme Boi added to the BTS line-up and Iron was named the de facto leader of the group.

But at this point BTS was nothing if not a fluid situation and, by the end of 2011, the group would be further in flux when both Iron and Supreme Boi left the group, citing reasons that, not surprisingly, were an anathema to the boy band training process, nonstop training that emphasized isolation and constant observation by the corporate powers and a desire for a less structured lifestyle in other groups and the goal of producing. i11even would follow the others out the door when he could not, creatively, get along with being in a boy band. It would not be long before Kidoh would also exit on the grounds that the time he was taking away from training to pass his college entrance exams did not fit in with the way of the boy band life. It was during this period that RM emerged as the leader of the group that was not yet what one would consider a full-fledged group. And that was starting to be of concern to the members who had already been in training for a while.

"New members were not being recruited so I felt anxious and restless," RM told *Sports Seoul.com*. "People around us kept asking 'When in the world are you debuting?'" J-Hope was beginning to have similar reservations as he offered to *BTS Trans.com*. "My friends and family asked when in the world I was going to debut. Whenever they did, I grew scared. I really wondered if BTS was training to never exist?"

The concept of Big Hit Entertainment was to always have other young talents in the pipeline and so Jungkook and V were soon added, with Jin and Jimin to follow shortly. By early 2012, BTS was finalized as RM, Suga, J-Hope, Jungkook, Jin, Jimin and V.

Now the real hard work would begin.

With the final line-up of BTS now set, Bang set about constructing the ideal training program for what he hoped would be future stars. One of his main influences when contemplating the BTS project was the 80's band Duran Duran whose selling point had always been a group of good looking guys who were also talented enough to make great music. Admittedly his hopes for what would be his version of Duran Duran were modest as he explained to *Soompi.com*. "When I first met the members of BTS, the goal wasn't for them to become international artists. I just thought that I could make something meaningful with this group."

While Bang was opting for a more freewheeling, less controlling training period, kind of like a regular school curriculum, he was, by degrees, borrowing, perhaps subconsciously, from the time-honored and, for Bang, despised culture of manufactured boy bands and their inherent restrictions. Almost from the beginning, stories would circulate, often from the group members themselves, of having their cell phones confiscated and prohibiting the members to date.

More in the open was the fact that the BTS trainees would typically spend ten to 15 hours a day honing their singing, dancing and songwriting skills and often would be getting by on only a few hours of sleep a night. And when they did sleep, it would be in a dormitory with the rest of the group, where they would learn the reality of their fellow dorm mates sleeping habits. Some snored. Some twisted and turned in their sleep. And some, owing to their erratic sleep habits, would wander in and out of the dorm room at all hours of the day and night.

However, the Big Hit Entertainment boss would always insist that he was attempting to build this group of seven teenagers into a well-oiled, professional and totally dedicated team of performers. "I didn't restrict them," he told *Soompi.com*. "I gave the group freedom from the start."

To the extent that each of the BTS members would be encouraged to develop both their strong and weak talents, often with hilarious and embarrassing results. As witness the time when everyone was encouraged to try their hand at rapping. Jimin chuckled as he told *Billboard* about his attempts at what, to him, was an alien art. "I went so far as to learn how to rap. But after they had me do it once, they were like 'let's just work harder on vocals.'"

But what the group found almost from the moment they entered what would be nearly three years of training was that there would be almost immediate pressure. Word along the K-Pop grapevine was that Bang was in the process of creating the ultimate K-Pop sensation which was dubbed in many corners as 'Bang Si-hyuk's Idols.' Expectations were high and the pressure was great on these young boys who skills entering the program were far from refined and much of what they would be learning would be foreign to them.

"Honestly, it was a lot of pressure," RM recalled to *BTS Trans.com*. "We had already gone through a lot of individual training to get to that point. But now our shoulders felt heavy from thinking we must become idols who won't let him [Bang] down, especially because he is such an outstanding figure who deserves a lot of respect."

The members of BTS proved to be highly motivated and avid pupils in the art of being pop stars. The seven boys became as brothers as the days and weeks of nonstop training continued well into 2012. Good or bad, they would have each other's backs and support each other in the most trying of moments. And there would be many of those.

RM, who the others regularly looked to as their leader for support and encouragement, acknowledged in *BTS Trans.com* that there were many times during the training that he just wanted to walk away. "There were many times during training that I wanted to give up. It was very difficult. During the time before the final lineup came together, J-Hope and I felt that we were neglected trainees. There were times I wanted to cry from the monotonous routine in the dorm and being away from my parents."

The inevitable routine of shuttling through the day and numerous instructors in the art of singing, choreography and performance routines would occasionally breed good natured teenage rebellion in the group.

While occasional days off from the training grind were allowed, the members of BTS quickly became aware that they were always being monitored and closely watched by Big Hit controllers on the lookout for even the slightest hint of 'acting out' that was not in synch with the Big Hit philosophy. One such moment came about the day when RM and another member of BTS snuck out to a nearby sweet shop and bought some ice cream, a no-no in the BTS weight-conscious training manual. They were walking down the street, ice cream in hand, when they sensed that they were being followed by a handler and immediately stuck the ice cream in their pockets. Sure enough, moments later they were approached by a Big Hit representative who questioned the boys as to whether they had been eating ice cream. They said no and, moments later, the Big Hit handler walked off. The ice cream was immediately out of their pockets and in their mouths.

As training continued, RM proved particularly adept when it came to skirting the rules when it came to food. "During my trainee days, it was really hard to stick to a diet," he confessed on the SBS variety show *Same Bed, Different Dreams*. "One day, I really wanted to eat jajangmyung [noodle soup] but I couldn't get caught by my agency. So, I pretended I had to go to the bathroom and snuck out to the neighborhood restaurant. I inhaled the jajangmyung in about two chopsticks' worth before I had to dash back."

While the endless days, weeks and months had succeeded in molding the young men into a professional polished performing unit, more importantly the time together had forged a seemingly unbreakable bond of trust and support during the often tension-packed and trying moments in their young lives. Suga broke down their concept of 'team support' in a straightforward manner when he told *Billboard,* "If there was a problem or someone had hurt feelings, we did not just leave it. We talked about it then and there."

As chronicled in *Metro UK* and the You Tube series *Burn the Stage*, J-Hope revealed that, at one point, the pressures of the training had become too much and he broke the news that he was leaving to the rest of the group. "I remember how Jungkook cried when I decided to leave. Jungkook and Jimin hugged and then we all cried together."

Things looked grim until RM recalled how the situation was resolved. "We couldn't have made it if you left. I can say this now. I talked to the guys. I told them we needed J-Hope. We couldn't make it without him. I tried really hard to convince them. I didn't want to think what would happen without them."

A long conversation took place with the rest of the group finally convincing J-Hope that he should stay. "I came back because I trusted the guys. We worked together for a long time. I came back because the members were there."

Much of the tension during the training period would often boil down to the group's feelings about their mentor, Bang Si-hyuk. Bang could be positive, supportive and encouraging to his charges. He could also come across as demanding and dictatorial. In particular, Suga would often chaff at much of his dealing with the Big Hit Entertainment boss and, in conversation with *BTS Trans.com*, recalled one particularly explosive moment.

"I resented Bang Si-hyuk. He's someone I respect but, at that time, I despised him. So one time, I left in the middle of practice and went to find Bang Si-hyuk to tell him I was quitting. I saw it like a bold declaration but, after a great bout of scolding, I ended up reluctantly walking back to the practice room. Back then my mind was narrow because all I ever did was practice. But, now that I look back on it, I think he had given us just the right amount of time. We got to make all the music we wanted during that period. I could say, because of this, BTS could exist."

By 2013, Bang felt BTS was ready. It was time to go forward and take on the music world. It was a sentiment echoed by RM who, in talking with *Time Magazine*, reflected on how seven young boys had gone through years of training and preparation and had now emerged as polished and poised performers. "We came together with a common dream to write and produce music that reflects our background as well as our life values of acceptance, vulnerability and being successful."

The creative operation was successful. The patient lived.

Chapter Six
There's Only One Way

Word spread quickly along the K-Pop Internet highway that Big Hit Entertainment's latest creation was about to be unveiled. There was a sense of excitement, mystery and, yes, cynicism about *BTS*. Bang's pedigree in the music industry could not be denied. But given the rollercoaster start to the company, even Bang's close friends had their doubts. And nobody was more aware of those doubts than Bang himself.

"Even the people around me didn't believe in me," he admitted to *Billboard*. "Even though they acknowledged that I had been successful in the past, they did not believe that I could take this boy group to the top."

When it came to encouraging creativity in the group, Bang was as good as his word, combining his own lyric writing skills with contributions from a number of group members and creating distinctive music with veteran K-Pop producers. Bang was forging a solid introduction to BTS with what would be their debut album, the nine song collection entitled *2 Kool 4 Skool*. The album, as exemplified by such tracks as "No More Dream" and "We Are Bulletproof, Part 2" showcased a promising first listen of dance-oriented hip-hop and K-Pop songs, love ballads and the first hints of breaking K-Pop constraints that were often topical in a way that few K-Pop groups rarely ventured.

The members of BTS were particularly proud of their songwriting contributions and were anxious to talk to *BTS Melon Showcase* about them. RM described "No More Dream" "as our title song. It's gangsta rap updated and revised with the emotion of 2013. It's a song that asks teenagers 'what is your dream?'" Suga described "Bulletproof, Part 2" as "an extension of a song we did in 2010 when we were trainees. It is a song that says we are the best and that we are full of spirit and that talks about the emergence of trap music."

Big Hit was going all out in preparation for the release. On May 21, the company launched a teaser countdown clock on the BTS website that was ticking down to the official release of *2 Kool 4 Skool*. Several promotional trailers and music videos were also created for the Internet. On June 12, 2013, Bit Hit Entertainment released *2 Kool 4 Skool* and the first single "No More Dream."

The album was an immediate success in Korea, peaking at No. 5 on Korea's *Gaon Album Chart*, selling an estimated 105,000 albums immediately upon release. Two singles "No More Dream" and "Bulletproof, Part 2" would follow in short order and would help solidify Bangtan Sonyeondan as the hot new group in Korea. To the group's way of thinking, it had all boiled down to a very simple formula, performance and message.

Big Hit's big promotional splash had been effective. So much so that the day after the release of *2*

Kool 4 Skool, the Bulletproof Boy Scouts made their very first live appearance on the Korean K-Pop chart television show entitled *M Countdown*. Backstage at the show, the members of the group were equal parts anxious, excited and nervous. Even those members who had already experienced performing live were feeding off adrenaline and anticipation.

When they were announced, the members of BTS raced onto the stage, churning in choreographed and synchronized dance steps amid flashing lights as they performed the songs "No More Dream" and "Bulletproof, Part 2" in a crisp, electrifying and emotional manner, immediately striking a sense of excitement in their audience. BTS completed their brief set to thunderous applause and screams. In a matter of minutes, BTS had defined what the group was all about. Off stage they were smiling broadly, tears of joy mixing with perspiration left over from their high energy performance. BTS was on its way.

Bang and Big Hit Entertainment were quick to capitalize on the success of *2 Kool 4 Skool* and almost immediately began prepping the second of what would be a trilogy of albums centered around the 2 Kool concept, *O!RUL8,2?* For a September 11. 2013 release. Promotion began in earnest with the clock countdown and a flurry of promotional video and audio trailers. But there would be something new.

In an attempt to further BTS*'s* exposure in other mediums, as well as to maximize the group's ease in front of a camera, the group created and starred in their very own variety show called *Rookie King Channel Bangtan* which would appear on *Korean MTV* starting September 3. The concept was simple: a fictional television program in which the group members would parody real Korean variety shows.

The result of the growing BTS mania and the good notices from the first album would result in an equally successful release of *O!RUL8,2?*. Like most second albums, BTS's follow up was a lyrically crisper and musically more diverse step up from the first, touching on some tantalizing rap and hip-hop influences while continuing to explore the ideals of teenagers finding their way in an often complex and restrictive world. *O!RUL8,2?* Would move steadily up the *Gaon Album Chart*, peaking at No. 4 and selling in excess of 120,000 copies.

BTS's popularity was growing at a lightning pace. With two albums out and receiving overwhelmingly positive notices, the group was closing in on the end of 2013 on a steady climb to the top of Korean celebrity. It was a fact that was reinforced at year's end when the group scooped up a total of five awards that included Best New Artist honors from the *Melon Music Awards* (their first official award), the *Golden Disc Awards* and, early in 2014, the *Seoul Music Awards*.

K Style would report that the members of BTS were literally speechless at the honors. J-Hope was joyous yet cautious. "The burden is great. I believe that the expectations of fans are getting even bigger. I also feel the responsibility of having to show increasing growth." V was at the other end of the emotional ride. "I could not believe it! I do not feel any real feeling yet. Is this true?"

Chapter Seven
All the Way Live

BTS were in a hurry.

Not merely satisfied to have the hot new group in Korea, Big Hit Entertainment was looking for nothing short of world domination. Their goal going into 2014 was, quite literally, to have it all. And by February 12, 2014, they were well on the way to having just that.

On that date, the final element of the group's *Skool* trilogy, *Skool Luv Affair* was released. Alternately smart and sassy, the album showcased maturing lyrical content from BTS that moved and grooved in a K-Pop way with the songs "Boy in Luv" and "Just One Day" offering up the ideal music odyssey for an audience that was attempting to find its way in life. That *Skool Luv Affair* would sell more than 200,000 copies in Korea was not a surprise. What was a surprise was that the album would also peak at No. 3 on *Billboard's World Album Chart*, a sure sign that the influence of BTS was spreading well beyond its Korean border.

BTS would find out just how far their popularity had spread in June 2014 when they were invited by the *Korean Cultural Ministry* to act as judges for a K-Pop cover dance competition in Moscow, Russia as part of the Bridge to Korea Festival, bringing Korean culture to foreign shores. The group was over the moon at the prospect of bringing their music to Russia and their experience would be chronicled with a seemingly endless number of tourist style selfies taken on the trip. The group took in some of the Russian sites and did a seemingly endless round of interviews with the magazines *K Plus* and *Onni*. Ever the troopers, the members of BTS attempted speaking Russian and, according to observers, received an A for effort from the Russian citizenry. The highlight of their Russian experience would be a performance by the group at an outdoor concert venue in front of an estimated 10,000 enthusiastic Russian music fans.

BTS had barely returned from their Russia trip when they raced back into the studio to record yet another album entitled *Dark & Wild*. The more cynical observers of the K-Pop industry were quick to speculate that BTS was now firmly entrenched in the business side of their music and that they were continuing to turn out new music at lightning speed ahead of a curve that would soon see the group fall from grace and be tossed aside by their fans in favor of the next big thing.

Those doomsayers may have had a point but the music coming out of the *Dark & Wild* sessions would end up being as daring if not more so than their predecessors. The formula may have seemed familiar, K-Pop style rough rap and hip-hop and the occasional sweet ballad, but it was clear that the tone of the new music was seemingly tougher and more determined. It was still K-Pop and still had the pop, commercial and largely inoffensive feel to it. But there were those subtle moments and the notion that creative chances were being taken.

Much of *Dark & Wild* was built on Bang's spirit of collaboration within BTS. RM, Suga and J-Hope had emerged as the primary lyricists and shared writing credit on most of the album's 14 tracks while Suga would take a co-producing credit on one song. As with the previous albums, *Dark & Wild* would benefit from a dizzying array of promotional videos and selected song releases that fully took advantage of the Internet and its various technological offspring. But once the album was completed, there would be no time to rest. For BTS, it was on to the next thing.

Which meant an extended working vacation in Los Angeles.

But what happened next may or may not have been a surprise. Shortly after their plane touched down in Los Angeles, the boys were surrounded by a goon squad of rough looking men who ushered them into a van and whisked them off to an unknown apartment location where they met rappers Coolio and Warren G. who would act as their teachers as BTS entered hip-hop high school and a two-week course in how to make it as a rapper in America. Enter the reality show *BTS: American Hustle Life*.

Over the course of eight episodes, *BTS: American Hustle Life* would instruct the young, wide-eyed group in the fine art of rapping and the African American culture that spawned it with instruction in different performance styles, hip-hop style dance moves, the art of beatbox and music and, in a graduation exercise, the group would actually write a song for Warren G. The admittedly far-fetched and often ridiculous contrivances

43

of the series were effectively padded out with BTS performances. As a camp, so bad it's good, reality romp, *BTS: American Hustle Life* was passable. As one long marketing tool for their upcoming album, it was pure gold.

While in Los Angeles, the band would make an appearance at the annual Los Angeles *KCon* Korean lifestyle and pop culture convention and would delight the audience with a performance. But with an eye toward showing that they had actually learned something during the making of *BTS: American Hustle Life*, the group had one final surprise in store for Los Angeles. Out of nowhere, BTS went on the Internet to announce that, in two days, they would be doing a free surprise show, entitled *BTS: Show and Prove*, at the world-famous Hollywood nightclub The Troubadour. A show that would be limited to an audience of 200.

As reported by the website *Kulturescene.com*, pandemonium greeted the announcement. Hundreds of K-Pop and BTS fans surrounded The Troubadour, with crowds spilling over into a nearby park. Tickets quickly disappeared but that did not stop hundreds of teens from hanging around in hopes of spotting the band coming in and out of the club.

Those fans lucky enough to get into the show were treated to BTS at the height of their talent, a show that swung from an early set proving that they had, indeed, learned something from their LA rapper teachers with a series of taut reworkings of some of their songs that emphasized their newly discovered American edge. The second half of the concert had BTS reeving up a series of by now familiar songs. The concert was a success on a number of levels, not the least of which was the fact that it was possible for seven boys to work their choreography and performance moves on a stage that was barely big enough for four.

With the conclusion of The Troubadour show, BTS had wrapped up their business in Los Angeles and returned to Korea where, literally on the day after their arrival, *Dark & Wild* would drop. The album immediately shot to the top of the charts, selling in excess of 200,000 copies, aided by creative videos and airplay for the album's two singles, "Danger" and "The War of Hormone." Big Hit knew they had a hit on their hands, especially when it came to Korea.

They were now encouraged to expand deeper into the Asian market, beginning with Japan which had a history of being a solid supporter of K-Pop music and artists and had proven particularly supportive of BTS. During the latter part of 2014, the group had released Japanese language versions of the songs "No More Dream," "Boy in Luv" and "Danger" between June and November and were more than a bit surprised when the combined sales of the singles totaled more than 100,000 copies. Sensing a strong second market in the making, Bang decided to record an all-Japanese language album for Japan to be released in December to test the overall market.

He also decided to take BTS out on their first full-fledged tour. Dubbed Live Trilogy II: The Red Bullet Tour, the tour would be rather leisurely in scope, three dates in Korea, three dates in Japan and one date each in The Philippines, Singapore and Thailand between October and November.

The very first show of the tour, before 5,000

screaming, adoring fans in Seoul, would not disappoint. Their 24-song set, spread out over two and a half hours, was the ultimate teenage party. BTS had prepared hard for this important first major concert and it showed as a multi-media backdrop of videos, lights and striking stagecraft served as the perfect sonic and visual setting for the group's emotional vocal and musical set. Tight, yet imaginative dance moves and an immediate and powerful give and take with their audience proved the perfect vehicle as the group raced through electrifying versions of their hits as well as notable album selections. BTS proved particularly masterful in mixing and matching their styles, rap, hip-hop, pop and all genres, into a seamless pattern of emotional set pieces that effectively presented high levels of emotion and presentation.

The members of BTS were exhausted and happy as they took their final bows at the conclusion of the show and raced off stage to screams and adulation from an appreciative audience. Backstage, the group was all smiles as they greeted the press, family, friends and business associates.

Reflecting on the performance a member of BTS (who was not named in an article by *NaverStarcast.com*) said, "We have thought that a singer is a real singer when performing a concert since our debut until now. Our hearts are full and happy since we feel like we have become a real singer since we held a concert like this today."

One night in Seoul had opened the door and truly bathed the band in the limelight. It would be the first of many such nights.

The group breezed through the remainder of 2014

on the wings of total adulation from audiences in Korea and Japan, their mixture of pop music and strong personal messages had struck an emotional nerve with young people, expressing their hopes, fear and, most importantly, the untold possibilities that awaited them. BTS had arrived as something more than just another flavor of the moment. In a short period of time, the group had become something much more important, a light and a spirit that gave their fans hope that their wildest dreams could truly come true.

The first half of the Live Trilogy tour ended in December 2014 on a high note. A crowd of more than 25,000 screaming fans was at the concert and pouring their hearts out as BTS performed what had, by this time, become their trademark, a full-blown spectacle of sight and sound.

After the show, BTS made time for the swarm of media that had become part of their backstage circus. *NaverStarcast.com*, in a quote not attributed to any particular band member, found the group to be eternally grateful for the professional and personal rise to the top of the K-Pop mountain. "We felt that we have taken our first step. We will present good songs and performances a lot in the future. So please always accompany us."

Chapter Eight
Making a Splash

Into 2015, BTS and Big Hit Entertainment had become a sensation in the K-Pop universe. The band's names, images and music were everywhere. But even for the best-known group on the planet, it was still just another day at the office. Jin offered up the typical BTS day in conversation with *K-Pop Starz.com*.

"We usually get ready in the morning, then go to the broadcasting station to do any interviews," he said. "Then we eat dinner and go to the practice studio. We practice together for a while and then some members will work on songwriting. After all this we go to sleep and then wake up and do it all over again."

J-Hope was more philosophical about the band's rise and success when he told *Amino.com* "It's a different world to the time when we were trainees. The feelings are completely different. It feels like our professional mentality is growing stronger and our beating hearts are still burning."

But for Big Hit CEO Bang Si-hyuk, the thoughts continued to be on the bottom line and what he could do to cultivate even more success and creativity. He was aware that some of the biggest groups in the history of popular music were creatively run by only one or two songwriters. The Beatles had Lennon and McCartney while The Rolling Stones had Jagger and Richards. But Bang did not see that as a plus when it came to BTS. And so, when, in early 2015, it came time to record their latest album, *The Most Beautiful Moment in Life, Part 1*, he made it plain to the members of the group that everybody would contribute to the writing and the production of the songs.

The group jumped at the creative opportunities they would all have and, as explained by RM in *K-Pop Starz.com*, they now had a rich pallet of influences to draw upon. "We watched movies and animation and some inspiration just came from experience. Our inspiration came from everything. It's hard to pinpoint one thing."

Big Hit Entertainment's Bang was a bit more circumspect in dissecting the new album. He saw the first *2 Kool 4 Skool* albums as a positive look at youth in rebellion. With the onset of *The Most Beautiful Moment in Life, Part 1*, he saw the group and the music making a hard creative turn into reality as he explained in *Soompi.com*. "What BTS does well is tell their own stories. In the case of *The Most Beautiful Moment in Life*, we did not want to glorify youth like we did in the previous albums. In reality, the youth of today are sad and painful and we should feel apologetic about the fact that they have to face this kind of world."

With *The Most Beautiful Moment in Life, Part 1* not scheduled to be released until April, the group used the time well with a short six date jaunt through Japan entitled Wake Up: Open Your Eyes from February 11-19. With stopovers in Tokyo, Osaka,

Nagoya and Fukuoka, BTS saw this as both an opportunity to pay back fans for their support and to prime the pump for the release of *The Most Beautiful Moment in Life, Part I.* The tour stops would be a mixture of old songs and a couple of previews of things to come in "Boyz with Fun" and "Converse High." All six dates for the min-tour sold out immediately and resulted in extra seats being added in a couple of venues and, in the case of the Fukuoka show, a series of live theater showings for those who could not get tickets. Equal parts concert extravaganza and good will tour, the *Wake Up: Open Your Eyes* tour succeeded on both counts.

When not performing or recording, the members of BTS were working just as hard on promoting their music. Their pro-marketing ways were much in evidence in the run up to the release of *The Most Beautiful Moment in Life, Part 1.* In typical Big Hit style, the promotion was very technological and Internet-focused in nature and aimed at the psyche of teenage consumers. Among the electronic come-ons were an animated and wildly surreal trailer featuring Suga doing an expansive and emotional rap over the album's title track. New photos were exposed as were alternate album cover designs done up in pink and white and a 120-page photobook was announced as an inclusion with the album. Along with the songs "Boyz with Fun" and "Converse High," which had already been unveiled in their live performances in Japan, Big Hit was also ratcheting up the expectation factor with the announcement that the first two singles off the new album would be "I Need U" and "Dope."

As the days counted down to the release of *The*

Most Beautiful Moment in Life, Part 1, BTS had the opportunity to listen to the album numerous times and, as such, became more intuitive about the changes in their music.

RM, in a *BTS Diary.com* interview, acknowledged the change when he said, "Rather than the endless beauty of youth, we were now attempting to illuminate the darker and heavier sides of youth." Suga seconded RM's thoughts during the same *BTS Diary* interview when he offered, "We included, in the music, the worries, concerns and thoughts that youth our age could have. All of our songs express commonly held concerns and fears." For his part, Jin told *BTS Diary* that the technical and emotional elements of their music had also changed. "In our last album, we had a really strong atmosphere in the songs of performance. But this time the mental choreography of the songs is dedicated to the idea of listening so the process was comfortable."

The promise of *The Most Beautiful Moment in Life, Part 1* would be realized with the April 29, 2015 release. The singles " I Need U" and "Dope" would spearhead a massive amount of interest, with the songs and accompanying music videos attracting listens and views in the millions. Sales of the album would ultimately reach over 200,000 copies, with massive support coming from Korea, China, Japan and Taiwan.

But, perhaps the biggest indication that BTS was truly poised to take over the world of music would come with an unprecedented assault on the vaunted *Billboard* charts. Six of the nine songs on the album— "I Need U," "Dope," "Hold Me Tight," "Boyz With Fun," "Converse High" and "Outro: Love Is Not

Over" would chart on the *Billboard World Digital Song Charts*. The album debuted at No. 2 on the *Billboard World Album Charts* and No. 6 on the *Billboard World Heatseekers Charts*.

Now all that seemingly remained was for BTS to once again take their music to the people and to hear J-Hope tell it, to *BTS Diary*, the group was ready to go. "Our anticipation is completely huge. We're nervous and anticipatory about meeting our fans."

Chapter Nine
BTS Meets World

Big Hit Entertainment was more than happy to oblige. The success of BTS up to that point had been perfect in its growth and execution. In a matter of two years, the group had risen from total unknowns to the hottest K-Pop act in the world. And in the grand scheme of things, the company was ready to showcase BTS on a worldwide scale.

Conceived as the second half of the *Live Trilogy II: The Red Bullet Tour*, BTS would spend three months touring the world. Between June 6 and August 29, the group would open their world to the rest of the world, with concerts in Kuala Lumpur, Sydney, Melbourne, Mexico, Brazil, Chile, Thailand and China. Sandwiched in between these international stops would be their formal introduction to fans in the United States with shows in Los Angeles, New York, Texas and Chicago.

There was initial concern that BTS would be venturing into territories not overly supportive of K-Pop acts but those fears were quickly dispelled. All the shows on the US portion of the tour sold out within five minutes of going on sale. The two Australian shows quickly sold out despite the fact that the country had a history of not being supportive of K-Pop acts. Likewise, Brazil, which had not shown much excitement over K-Pop, had to relocate the show to a larger arena because of a huge demand for tickets.

The group had long ago become accustomed to the notion that their live performances would be as much a physical exercise as creative experience and, in preparation for the upcoming tour, focused on the physical aspect of their performance, according to RM who told *My Metro.com* "To get a good stamina while performing on stage, we work out every day. We spend a lot of time on that."

The show presented to the world was now polished. The group's lightning like vocal delivery, their choreography and an all-around enthusiasm for the experience they were presenting to their fans continued to be the cornerstone of the BTS performance. The proverbial icing on the cake was a state of the art technological backdrop that consisted of lights, videos and a smartly surreal stage experience that emphasized the message of the songs as well as their entertainment value. By the time June 6 rolled around, all systems were go.

Kuala Lumpur, Malaysia was an ideal first stop. The estimated 3,000 fans in attendance were enthusiastic and, of equal importance, familiar with BTS and their music. In response, the group gave its audience a tantalizing retrospective of their familiar songs, some between song patter and an overall concert experience that was as international in spirit as it was adhering to the K-Pop brand of entertainment.

What was evident in their performance was the humble and totally appreciative feelings they had toward their fans. Real rather than calculating, the gratitude the band expressed that night, and on all future nights, was totally heartfelt and endearing. A prime example being RM's thank you at the conclusion of their Malaysia show, "You are all the best. Without you we are not here. We love you and Malaysia. The support you give us is another wonderful memory."

By the time BTS touched down in Australia for the July 10 and 12 shows in Sydney and Melbourne, the show had evolved into a precise and very fast program of songs, choreography and video effects. To some observers, the show almost seemed too rote and by the numbers but the group managed to inject just the right amount of emotion and angst to get their messages across. Of particular note, BTS used the occasion of the Australian shows to engage in the risky take of speaking English throughout the entire set. Not surprisingly, RM was the most fluent but the other members of BTS did their best and managed to use their halting English to humorous effect.

BTS left Australia in a euphoric state. The band and the specifics of the show were in a good place and would continue a steady course. The band was in a state of both exhaustion and euphoria as they hopped a plane that would take them to the other side of the world. What they did not realize was that their first serious bit of controversy was also on board.

During an Australian press conference, RM made what seemed to be an innocuous, joking comment. "Well, when I first met V and J-Hope, I couldn't see them because they were so black. So yeah, when the night gets dark, I couldn't find them." There would be some grumbling on the Internet that RM's remarks were racist. But the dust up appeared to pass without much notice.

Next stop America.

New York City was everything the boys could hope for. Larger than life. Glamorous. Theater marquees blazing with hope, dreams and untold potential. It was in the city that never sleeps that BTS would make their stand.

The sold-out show would present some pleasant surprises. In typical K-Pop fashion, BTS started out a highly choreographed and extremely polished vocal stance. Creatively, the first few songs were picture-perfect without a performance hair out of place. But then something unexpected happened. The group suddenly launched into a completely different place that would continue throughout the remainder of the show. They were suddenly more freestyle and less by the numbers. Vocally, they were not just sounding like their records, adding smart and unexpected interplay that added punch to even their most laidback songs. Likewise, disciplined choreography suddenly gave way to seemingly improvised and acrobatic choreography. Reality and fun-loving riffs and surprises were suddenly the order of the day and the sold-out crowd was eating it up.

Backstage, the group's management was suddenly concerned.

During the course of the show, a rash of death threats against RM began playing out across the Internet. The most ominous being, "I just bought my gun. It's about to go down. RIP." Management made the decision to abruptly cut the show short, shortly after BTS emerged for what was normally a multiple song encore. After one song, the group waved goodnight and walked off the stage, leaving a perplexed audience wondering what was going on.

In the aftermath of the threats, New York police had descended on the concert hall, adding to the surreal nature of the moment. The band's normal after-show meet and greet with a select group of fans had been cancelled as well. An unexpected, dark side of the Internet celebrity universe had suddenly become a part of BTS's world view. But the boys were not about to cave in to threats and would almost immediately push fear and suspicion out of their minds. The US tour was now on to Texas.

Heading into the Midwest, with stops in Dallas and Chicago, appeared on the surface to present the most challenges. Known, primarily for their adherence to rock and roll, blues and country, it was a mystery as to how much support there would be for a group of young teen boys and their brand of pop music. But one needed only look at the lines around the concert halls and the fans' unbridled mania for their newly minted pop heroes to know that BTS and the concept of K-Pop knew no boundaries.

BTS cruised into Los Angeles for their final stop on the US portion of the tour at the top of their game. Touring to this extent had honed their performance skills to a knife's edge. BTS were admittedly tired and with the inevitable rounds of press and last-minute sound checks, sleep of any length had become a plus. But they were seven young men in their moment and adrenaline and the adulation of screaming fans would get them through the night. Their faces were triumphant in the aftermath of the LA show. Soon the City of Angels would be in their mental rearview mirror and it was on to the rest of the world.

The band's arrival in Mexico was the pop culture equivalent of the conquest of a new land. Fans had been kept abreast of the group's arrival plans on a constant basis thanks to the Internet and the result was that the airport was filled with hundreds of screaming young fans when the band's plane taxied to a stop. The concert itself was a predicted success but it was more evidence that BTS was well on the way to conquering the world. No longer simply a K-Pop act with only regional impact, BTS was now officially a universal attraction. This kind of fan mania continued throughout their jaunt through Latin America with stops in Brazil and Chile where fans reportedly had spent 20 days living in tents near the concert venues awaiting the arrival of the band.

August 2015 saw the *Live Trilogy* tour coming to an end with shows in Thailand and Hong Kong. There was a sense of nostalgia mixed with the BTS sense of theatrics and bombast that had become the trademark of their concerts and their impact on the world. The statistics of the *Liv Trilogy Tour Episode 1 and 2* had been staggering. *BTS* had touched down in 18 cities in 13 countries and had performed in front of an estimated 80,000 fans. That the tour had been immensely profitable and had made Big Hit Entertainment very happy. For Bang Si-hyuk, it was validation that he and his company had arrived as a legitimate player in the K-Pop game. It would be a tour that BTS would look back upon fondly.

"Our overseas tour was a long journey," RM told a *Scoompi.com* journalist. "It was an extremely touching experience. We were amazed when international fans would sing along to all of our songs."

But for BTS, taking their final bow at the conclusion of their Hong Kong performance, the important thing had been the support of the fans and, for that, they would be eternally grateful. And it was to the fans that they spoke directly.

"Finally, BTS's first world tour has ended," the group collectively said amid the cheers and screams for more. "Thank you so much for those who came to meet us. Hope to see you soon. Love you."

Chapter Ten
Free Time? What Free Time?

Free time? What's that?

The reality is that the members of BTS don't really have much of it. Between recording, touring, rehearsing and promoting, there are not nearly enough hours in the day and luxury for the biggest group on the planet is usually a few hours' sleep. But the members of BTS do, occasionally, get some time to themselves and, thanks to the information hosted on *Quora, Koreaboo* and *Korea Portal*, the group has reported what they like to do when their lives are not all about the business of being pop stars.

Rather than fall into the predictable party hard lifestyle of the majority of celebrities, BTS use their off time to act like your everyday young adults, who like to shop, take trips and play video games. When it comes to the constantly changing gaming world, all of the group members are up on the latest challenges, with Jin and V big fans of the game *Overwatch*. Jin, V and RM are big on travel. Their travel plans regularly include trips to Jeju, Japan and Europe. The group members regularly use their free time to reconnect with their families.

Jin is quite the fisherman and, when time permits, he goes fishing with his father. When he is home,

Jungkook usually heads for the pile of mail that has built up in his family's house. "I have a lot of packages and mail stacked up and I want to hurry and open it." For his time off, V has developed into quite the photographer. "I like to travel and take photos of everything I see."

When RM is away from BTS, his interest is immediately drawn to his ever-growing collection of toys, an experience that often borders on the mystical. "I want to organize my action figures that I've collected," he reflected. "I want to heal my mind while looking at them. It would be nice to have that state of body and mind that I am aching for and to have that kind of good cheer."

But when it gets right down to it, the members of BTS are always, instinctively, drawn to the simple lives they had before they became superstars and that means going home. Which for J-Hope means returning to familiar, sights, sounds and people. "Going home and getting some rest is the big thing for me. I get to play with my puppy and to eat my mom's cooking."

Chapter Eleven
Pack Your Bags

BTS barely had time to unpack their bags at the conclusion of their first world tour before they were hard at work on their fourth collection of music, an EP entitled *The Most Beautiful Moment in Life, Part 2.* At a time when many expected a greatest hits package would be put together to give the group time to, creatively, catch their breath, BTS had already decided that the next album would flex some mighty philosophical muscle and messages.

As indicated by the album's title, *The Most Beautiful Moment in Life, Part 2* would be a continuation of the complexities of youth entering life and dealing with the real world, a rather ambitious approach in a K-Pop world populated by lighter than air and predictable songs. The group acknowledged in a 2015 interview with *Soompi.com* that the song "Run" typified the vibe and social attitude they were trying to convey.

"*Part 2* is the second part of our two-part youth story," explained RM. "The songs are about youth. *Part 1* explained how youth was tiring and difficult and it also touched on how we feel like we're always on edge. *Part 2* will have a more adventurous and daring feel to it. It's natural that people fail or make mistakes but I think it's a touchy subject for society as a whole. So we wanted to comfort ourselves by saying one mistake or failure is not the end of the world."

RM continued, insisting that BTS did not want to take the easy way out when it came to their music. "We didn't want to just blankly say 'cheer up' or 'be strong.' We really wanted to comfort people our way by producing the music and writing the lyrics ourselves."

The perceived new maturity and worldliness of BTS come to the band quite naturally. Given the freedom of expression offered by Big Hit Entertainment, BTS had been, surprisingly so by K-Pop standards, outspoken in their attitudes and beliefs about real world issues. The group, collectively, and RM in particular, had publicly come out in support of gay rights. RM has also been upfront in dealing with his own mental health issues, proclaiming in an interview with *Kpopism.com* when he offered, "I have light and dark issues and I am not always happy."

Consequently, the boldness on *The Most Beautiful Moment in Life, Part 2* songs is not surprising. The themes of the songs are alternately contemplative, emotional and upfront, especially when it comes to addressing life issues. But the music itself remains very pop and accessible in a tried and true K-Pop sense. Much of this maturity is the result of the freedom proffered by Big Hit Entertainment and its CEO Bang Si-hyuk.

"It's true BTS has tried a variety of different things," Bang has told journalists. "But I don't think they've changed. Their music is the expression of their earnest and candid mind. I think we must not meddle in their music. BTS's own intention is the most important thing."

There would be the usual round of promotion and video teases for the new album, including, on September 8, the release of a 12-minute short that would encapsulate the essence of the upcoming album as well as three concert appearances in Seoul, South Korea, going under the title *The Most Beautiful Moments in Life, Part 2 On Stage Tour*, whose set list would include a handful of new songs from *The Most Beautiful Moments in Life, Part 2*.

The concerts would unveil a new level of BTS performance, a first being a live band that would add to the substance of the newer songs, and a higher degree of progressive choreography. The three concerts would sell out immediately after their announcement, which, even at their current level of popularity, surprised the band.

During a press conference promoting the tour and reported by *Soompi.com*, RM admitted, "I was very surprised. I'm happy that we keep having sold-out concerts, especially as we keep moving on to larger venues."

The sold-out shows in Seoul were evidence that BTS was easily the most professional and exciting group on the K-Pop scene. Old favorites and new songs alike took on a new level of passion and importance, something the die-hard fans never seemed to tire of. Surprises in the pace and structure and the extravagant staging of the show indicated that the members of BTS now had a firm grip on what the audience wanted and were capable of delivering their message laden songs with strength and believability.

BTS were thrilled with the response to their Korean return and would acknowledge the crowd at the conclusion of the final Korean concert when they told the audience, "We are back in concert in Korea after so long. We missed you. We missed your shouting and screaming. We are so happy."

The impact of the Korean shows took on even more importance 24 hours after the last of the Seoul shows when *The Most Beautiful Moment in Life, Part 2* was officially unveiled.

The success of *The Most Beautiful Moments in Life, Part 2* had already been assured with pre-orders on the album passing 150,000 copies days before its official release. The video for the album's first single, "Run," had already been viewed more than two million times. The demand for BTS to perform live had reached manic proportions around the world and so a second leg of *The Most Beautiful Moments in Life, Part 2 Onstage Tour* were added with shows in Japan.

The first three shows on the Japan leg of the tour were mirror images of the Korean shows. The group was performing at an extremely high physical and emotional level. It had always been speculated that the group of such young men might be pushing themselves too hard and that there was the ever-present possibility of physical or emotional breakdown. BTS and Big Hit Entertainment insisted that the group members were in perfect shape and more than capable of performing at a consistently high level. But something happened on December 27, literally hours before a scheduled performance in Kobe Japan that would change all that.

The group was in the midst of rehearsing for that night's performance when suddenly Suga and V felt dizzy and had to sit down. The rehearsal came to an immediate halt and the two boys were whisked off to a nearby hospital for an emergency checkup. CT scans were performed and, while the results indicated that nothing was clinically wrong, the doctors warned that any physical activity during the course of a performance might cause them to feel dizzy again and recommended that both Suga and V stay in the hospital for further observation. While Suga and V insisted they were well enough to do that night's performance, cooler heads at Big Hit decided that it would be best for the pair to stay in the hospital and get well.

There was talk that BTS might go on as planned, minus the two ailing members, but that was quickly dismissed because it would not present a true representation of the group. Finally, the decision was made to cancel both the Kobe shows and return to Korea where Suga and V would go through a thorough medical examination. The two BTS members would soon be given a clean bill of health and the group would return to Kobe for two make-up shows in late March 2016.

BTS returned home in late March to find that *The Most Beautiful Moments in Life, Part 2* had become their break-through album on a number of fronts. "Run" became their first song to debut at #1 on all the important real time digital charts. All nine tracks on the EP would enter the *Gaon Weekly Album Charts*. But the impact in the Korean market was to be expected. What remained the biggest success story was the impact the album had on the international market.

A total of eight tracks from *The Most Beautiful Moments in Life, Part 2* entered the *Billboard World*

Digital Songs Charts literally at the same moment. Furthering their impact on the North American market, the album debuted at #171 on the *Billboard Top 200 Album Charts*. The final question of BTS's internationally was answered when *The Most Beautiful Moment in Life, Part 2* landed high on the *Billboard International Album Charts*, where it would remain for 22 weeks.

But the members of BTS had little time to relish the commercial victory. In a matter of weeks, they were once again packing their bags and returning to the road.

Chapter Twelve
Lost in the Moment

And the reason for BTS's quick return to touring had much to do with the fact that yet another album, *The Most Beautiful Moment in Life: Young Forever*, was already on the horizon. What had initially been conceived as the third and final element of the *Most Beautiful Moment in Life* trilogy, consisting of all new material, had morphed into a massive compilation.

Young Forever, in its final form, now consisted of all 23 tracks from the previous *Beautiful Moment* EP's, several remixes of selected songs and a handful of brand new singles, "Epilogue," "Young Forever," "Fire" and "Save Me." This was a mature and assured album, as fitting the third of the trilogy, a deep and insightful look at youthful doubts and fears as reflected in both the most private moments of BTS and their fans wrapped up in a hopeful and promising future. Lyrically and musically as substantial as K-Pop can be, *The Most Beautiful Moment in Life: Young Forever* was easily in the tradition of all great bands who finally took that all important step from novelty to legitimacy.

RM, always seemingly in a constant state of deep thought, was, likewise, deep in thought when discussing the levels of understanding that permeated *Young*

Forever and the previous *Beautiful Moment* collections with *Affinity.com.*

"Everyone says that we are all in our most beautiful moments. We really are but we wanted to look at the real meaning behind that. So many young people are suffering, trying to get jobs and are giving up lots of things. But even in that transition period, one can think that happiness is something you have to achieve. One can still feel happy during the process of achieving something. Maybe it's a period of time when something big happens. If one knows and feels this moment truthfully and one is ready to accept that moment, then the entire life can be beautiful."

BTS was forthcoming in saying that the final album in the *Beautiful Moment* trilogy was, creatively and emotionally, some of the most trying times they had experienced in their career to date. Jin offered up as much in conversation with *Soompi.com* when he said, "Last year we unveiled *Part 1* and *Part 2* and now we've wrapped up the trilogy. We've been doing it for a year so we have been both excited and nervous. It was a new feeling." J-Hope chimed in during that same interview, waxing nostalgic at the completion of the trilogy. "It also feels a little sad. We've been working hard and steady for a year and now we're at the end."

The ability of BTS to expand their creative horizons and to progress within the often-stifling K-Pop machine continued to pose the question of the relationship between the group and Big Hit Entertainment's Bang Si-hyuk. The freedom the band has often seems unbelievable to observers. Which is why in interviews, such as one conducted by *Soompi*

69

during BTS's *Epilogue tour*, BTS would acknowledge that their relationship was too good to be true.

Suga acknowledged that, "He (Bang) has the style to let us do what we want. In the case of the title track from *Young Forever*, it's hard because the title track has to stick in your ear and the melody has to be good. But we received a lot of good advice about producing from Hyuk. However, he doesn't touch B side tracks and mixtapes. He is rational and not coercive."

Jimin echoed Suga's sentiments. "Hyuk makes an effort to communicate with us so he shares a lot of stories. We are close but sometimes it's hard because he has a strong force. But at the end of the day, this is really a company that feels like a family."

Despite what many in the industry considered a short promotion time for the album, although the bells and whistles of a typical BTS promotion were much in evidence, the album proved an immediate hit. An estimated 300,000 copies of *Young Forever* sold in pre-sale well ahead of the May 2 release. As always, videos played as a primary marketing tool, especially when it came to the newer songs. The video for "Fire" became the fastest BTS video to reach one million views, in just six hours, and would reach ten million views in 75 hours. The songs "Fire," "Save Me" and "Epilogue: Young Forever" debuted in the top three spots on the *Billboard World Digital Charts* while the group continued its march on US audiences, with the album debuting at No. 107 on the important *Billboard Top 200 Album Charts*.

Five days after the release of *The Most Beautiful Moment in Life: Young Forever*, BTS were once again on the road with *The Most Beautiful Moment in Life: Epilogue Tour*. Like their previous world tour, the *Epilogue* tour would showcase BTS on a massive sale. The group would once again use a live band for much of their performance and expansive new videos that would be an important element for much of their show were filmed. The "All-Asia" tour would consist of 14 concerts between May and August with stops in in South Korea, Taiwan, China, Japan, The Philippines and Thailand and would consist of selections from all three *Beautiful Moment* albums.

The tour kicked off with two sold-out performances in the Olympic Park Gymnastic Arena in South Korea. As always, expectations were high and anticipation for yet another BTS performance were at a fever pitch. BTS did not disappoint.

The integration of music, message and technological delights meshed in a synchronized, polished manner. The idea of playing the *Beautiful Moment* music in chronological order across three albums had been an ambitious one to start and watching as BTS was able to pull it off in such an exciting and seamless manner had the audiences of both shows cheering the band on at every turn. BTS could feel the waves of emotion from the crowd and it succeeded in driving them forward to frenetic concert perfection and abandon. This was a truly powerful moment for the band, another nostalgic look to their past and on into the future.

RM expressed as much in an after-concert interview with *News Everyday.com* when he emotionally expressed how BTS was in a state of bliss. "Our dreams before were to become a number one group on music programs and to become stars. Our perspectives have changed. It's good to be modest but it's also important to enjoy this moment. It's not good to waste this joyful youth and music with anxiety and fear."

The sheer scope of a typical BTS show continued to test the physical and emotional stamina of the group. The fact that the members were young and physically healthy had always kept the concerns for their wellbeing to a minimum and the *Epilogue* tour was not showing any signs of fatigue or distress until BTS reached Beijing, China at the midway point in the tour and everything was running true to form.

When suddenly it became apparent that RM was having trouble breathing.

The heat in Beijing coupled with the heavy costumes they were wearing resulted in RM suffering an unexpected heatstroke. There was the immediate sense on stage that something was wrong. RM left the stage and was treated by the ever-present medical team while the remainder of BTS carried on without him for the rest of the show. News spread internationally about RM's episode and the rapper was quick to update the world via tweet the next day, as reported by the *K-Pop Herald*. "I am sorry to cause you all trouble, especially to my Chinese fans, for not being able to show my best. I am a lot better now."

At this point in the *Epilogue* tour, BTS were automatic in the way they handled the day to day activities that culminated in their nightly performances in front of thousands. But it became evident, during those rare, quiet moments that the members were philosophically in different places when it came to performing live.

"I always have fun and feel happy on stage," Jimin reflected to *Scoompi*. "I could feel that more people are supporting us through this tour compared to the last one. I think that means we have to work that much harder and continue to improve." Jungkook proved more tentative on the subject in the *Scoompi* interview when he said, "I am always nervous and thankful every time I go up on stage. It's hard during the moments when we perform difficult choreography but, when the concert ends, the audience ends up giving us more strength."

BTS returned home at the conclusion of the *Epilogue* tour in an emotional state of grace. The tour and the now concluded *Beautiful Moment* trilogy had been absolute proof that BTS were not just another fly by night cog in the K-Pop machine. They were now a legitimate musical entity, one whose creativity could not be denied. The individual members of the group were now dealing with emotions and prospects for a real future and who were now attempting to come to grips with they had become.

Jin was in a state of abject joy with the conclusion of the *Beautiful Moment* odyssey. "It's beyond my expectations. Honestly, I couldn't predict that we would receive this much love from so many people. Sometimes I think about it suddenly before falling asleep. I'm so happy that we are receiving this overwhelming amount of love."

Suga saw it as a success that would, hopefully, bring more success. "There is pressure beyond the *Most Beautiful Moment in Life* trilogy. I think that there are no times when I don't feel that pressure. I think we will always have to put forth music that's

73

better than our last. Our next album and the ones following it are all important albums to us and we are working hard to make them even better."

Suga would finally wax philosophical in defining BTS's present and future. "I think if there's a start, there's also an end. Personally, I think *Young Forever* is an album that I will never forget for the rest of my life. But if you stay stagnant in the same place, then rotting occurs. We will come back with even better music and concepts to be able to say goodbye to *The Most Beautiful Moment in Life*.

"Beautifully."

Chapter Thirteen
Time Off for Creative Behavior

To say that the members of BTS are workaholics is only half the story.

Yes, they work hard and the nature of BTS is that they work literally 24/7. But of greater importance is that the individual members are also creatively hot-wired to the world around them. Ideas and influences can come from anywhere and at any time. Which is why when on tour, the most important element of their packing is recording equipment that can be set up and utilized during a moment of inspiration, any time day or night.

Suga gave *Grazia Magazine* an idea of what creating on the road was like when he offered, "I'll be in the hotel room. I unpack my equipment. I set it up so I can do everything from the hotel between performances."

BTS are not big partiers. What they are is explorers, searching their minds and taking in outside forces to forge both group and individual identities.

And those traits were very much in evidence during those hectic, around the clock recording years of 2015-2016 when the individual members were putting out a wide variety of solo and non *BTS* centric projects.

RM

RM returned to his rap roots when away from BTS activities. Fueled by influences from the group's time filming their reality series in Los Angeles, RM was especially influenced by legendary rapper Warren G and, in March 2015, cemented that relationship when he combined with G on a single called "Please Don't Die" which showcased RM's talents taking a rougher, very street stance on the subject of dealing with haters in an Internet world. During this period, he joined forces with hip-hop artists EE and Dino to form a one off hip-hop project called *MFBTY,* collaborating on the songs "Bucku Bucku" and "Bang Diggy Bang Bang" and appearing in front of the camera in their respective videos. RM also found time to do a feature bit on the *Primary* EP track "U."

But it would remain for the March 2015 release of his first solo mixtape, entitled *RM*, to cement the at large impression of his own individual voice. RM played things smart on his debut solo disc. The songs take rap, soul, blues and all manner of the black music experience and funnel it through a musical attitude that, while owing some moments to the BTS way of creating, was heavy on experimentation and a respect for traditional musical forms. *RM* would mark RM as somebody who can make something special out of his own mind and imagination.

RM continued to expand his skills into what many perceived as the mainstream arena. Most notably was the August release of the single "Fantastic" from the movie soundtrack *Fantastic Four* in which he collaborated with singer Mandy Ventrice and what many considered a giant step in his songwriting and production collaboration with

Big Hit Entertainment's Bang Si-hyuk on *Homme's* single "Dilemma."

Suga

Suga's lone side project during this period was a brave and thoughtful exploration in his debut mixtape which was released in August 2016 on Soundcloud. The recording, which was released under the title *August D* rather than his own name, was a deliberate and raw departure from BTS and K-Pop conventions as well as something very personal and private, a candid look at his own personal demons as the ten tracks on *August D* address the issues of depression, OCD and social phobia as well as a very progressive philosophy of dreaming and yet not dreaming.

Suga's examination of the challenges of living in a world not so kind was such a radical departure from BTS that he went the Soundcloud route rather than issuing *August D* as a conventional Big Hit studio album. "I really like to talk about dreams, youth and reality," he offered during a conversation with *Grazia*. "It's a social atmosphere. Having your own dreams is a difficult environment in itself. People are frustrated because they don't see the future. I hope that people who listen to my music will be comforted."

August D would end 2016 on the prestigious list of *Fuse* TV's Top 20 Mixtapes of the Year.

Jungkook

When Jungkook put BTS on hold, it was for the purpose of exercising both his music and acting muscles. When it came to music, he was very much a fan boy, doing covers of songs by Justin Bieber, Adam Levine, David Guetta and Korean artists Zion T, Roy Kim and Lee Hi that appeared on several Internet platforms. In a bit of homage to fellow BTS member Suga, Jungkook teamed with fellow group member Jimin to do an alternative version of the song "So Far Away" from Suga's *August D* mixtape.

He was equally active in Korean television, cast in the pilot episodes of the series *Flower Crew* and *Bromance* and making guest appearances in episodes 71 and 72 of the series *King of Mask Singer* as the character 'fencing man."

J-Hope

What J-Hope was doing during this time away from the public eye would test the mettle of any detective. He was keeping things fairly low key. J-Hope co-hosted a couple of Korean television shows, *Inkigayo* and *Show Music Corps* and it was later reported that he did some behind the scenes promotional videos for an upcoming BTS album. But beyond those tidbits, it was all a deep dark secret.

Jin

Jin addressed his non BTS projects more with an eye toward having fun. Besides the aforementioned pairing with Jimin on the Suga song "So Far Away," he also teamed up with fellow BTS buddy V for the song "It's Definitely You" as their contribution to the soundtrack to the monthly Korean television drama *Hwarang: The*

Poet Warrior's Youth. Left to his own devices, Jin did a pair of covers of the songs "Mom" by *RA.D* and "I Love You" by Mate. For Jin, recording that song was deeply personal as he explained in a *Koogle TV*.com interview. "I really wanted to share my voice and I've been preparing for a long time. It was difficult because the preparation was like for an album. But I wanted to relay how I felt with a great song so I worked really hard on this."

Jimin

Likewise, Jimin was keeping his non-BTS activities low key. Putting music aside, he appeared on a number of Korean television shows that included *The Workplace of God*, *Hello Counselor* and *Please Take Care of My Refrigerator*. He also hosted the music programs *Show Music Corps* and *M Countdown*.

V

V ended up doing double duty on *Hwarang: The Warrior Poet's Youth*. Besides his previously mentioned soundtrack contribution with Jin on "It's Definitely You," V also made his professional acting debut on an episode of the show. His credits were under his real name, Kim Tae-hyung.

Chapter Fourteen
Wings Take Flight

With their meteoric rise and nothing really left to prove, 2016 would have been the time to relax, take a few months off to recharge their creative energy and, to appease the gods of K-Pop economy, release a stop-gap live album or a collection of greatest hits and a handful of never released songs from the vaults. The last things most observers of the K-Pop scene expected was that BTS would take the occasion to release their riskiest and most ambitious project to date, a truly progressive and forward-thinking experiment called *Wings*.

In conception, *Wings* appeared light years more mature than any previous BTS effort, a truly massive and inter-personal look at the concepts of temptation and growth. That the group's influence drew largely on the very adult writer Herman Hesse and his novel *Demian* was a clue that the perception of BTS as this cutesy and largely inconsequential group of pre-fab pop stars was about to be stood on its head. But the real step forward for BTS would come from the group being allowed to totally go it alone.

RM reflected on the maturity of the *Wings'* philosophy in a conversation with *Korea Portal* when

80

he explained how, "Each song reflects on the hardships we overcame. It really represents the people we are."

While the lead single, "Blood, Sweat & Tears," was very much in the BTS mold musically, the creative concept for *Wings* was almost immediately opened up to let the individual members of BTS be their own force. There would be seven solo songs, one for each member, while six of the seven songs crediting the members of *BTS* as writers and producers of their own material. There had been hints of BTS solo efforts with the mixtapes of RM and Suga but *Wings* would stake claim to being the first full blown studio album to allow the group members to do their own thing.

There were concerns that such an effort might lead to unevenness of the album with some songs working while others would not be as successful. Egos might be hurt. The potential for disharmony in the group was a possibility. Bang Si-hyuk, in *Soompi.com*, insisted that the opportunities for growth in *Wings* was worth the gamble.

"I don't think the results of *Wings* was a matter of luck," said Bang. "The members of BTS have steadily taken steps and they are showing the results of their continuous growth. I made a promise to BTS that I would help them become an established team and to do their best with their individual responsibilities."

The *Wings'* production was, by degrees, often daunting and nerve wracking as BTS members were regularly called upon to contribute to other people's songs. During a post-production press conference, RM was the guide to some of the ups and downs of creating *Wings*. Stepping in to write lyrics for Jungkook's song "Begin" proved a particularly grueling challenge. "At first I was hesitant and unsure of writing as if I was Jungkook. To speak from his perspective when I am not him was a confusing and uncertain task."

Regarding Jimin's song "Lie," he was complimentary in a sort of back-handed way. "He really killed it with his lyrics. I had no idea he wrote it himself because it was so good." He was intellectually focused when he described the deeper meaning of the song "Blood, Sweat & Tears." "The harder a temptation is to resist, the more you think about it and vacillate. That uncertainty is part of the process of growing. 'Blood, Sweat & Tears' is a song that shows how one thinks, chooses and grows."

But amid the pre-release hype, RM would turn reflective, in an *MSO* pre-tour interview when he put the challenges of *Wings* in their most simple form. "The new songs are about us, our friends and our loved ones. I think of them as conversations with my close friends. All the new tracks have distinctive colors, tones and stories."

With an October 10 release date on the horizon, Big Hit Entertainment wasted no time getting the word out. Beginning in late August, a flood of promotional song trailers and music videos were slamming every conceivable Internet site, building the level of suspense and anticipation among the fans.

It was during this period that BTS managed to unwind from the pressures of creating *Wings* by sneaking out yet another album, specifically for the fans in Japan entitled *Youth*. An amalgam of 13 older songs and obscure titles, nine of which were sung in Japanese, *Youth* proved a solid hit, selling 44,000 copies on the day of release early in September. The album would be certified gold and would go on to sell in excess of 100,000 copies.

October 9 would be the official unveiling of *Wings* in a live show for fans that featured much of the new material. Good vibe. The fans were frantic with excitement. The new songs went down well. The pre-release publicity had done its job.

Well before the official release date, *Wings* had already sold more than 500,000 pre-sale date copies. With the official release, related elements the album would also benefit. The music video for the first single, "Blood, Sweat & Tears" would set a new record for the fastest K-Pop video to reach ten million views. *Wings* was an immediate success in the group's home country, with the album, simultaneously holding the No. 1 position on all of the South Korean sales charts. The album would continue making inroads with US audiences, charting at No. 26 on the *Billboard Top 200 album* charts. All told, *Wings* would sell an astounding 100,000 physical copies within two weeks of its release.

RM recalled the moment he received the news in an *Orange County Register* interview and how it was too good to be true. "Somebody in the company sent me a message," he said. "It said, 'You got No. 26 on *Billboard*. OMG congratulations.' At first, I thought, 'Ha ha, your humor isn't really very good.' We didn't believe it. But when more messages started coming in, we realized that it was no joke. When we heard that and really got that it was real, I was saying 'Ok, this is going to be a whole other world.'"

That BTS's more serious turn was successful was only matched by the critical raves from major music and pop culture press. *Fuse* greeted the album with "The rising K-Pop phenoms' new album is doing it right by letting their seven members spread their artistic wings and solidifying their individual identities." In a similar tone, *Rolling Stone* proclaimed *Wings* "One of the most conceptually and sonically ambitious pop albums of 2016."

To this point, BTS had managed to survive the curse of oversaturation with a seemingly endless series of top-flight music. Going into 2017, and only three months removed from the release of *Wings*, BTS were at it again, testing the insatiable appetite of their fans with yet another album entitled *You Never Walk Alone*. *You Never Walk Alone* was essentially a repackaging of *Wings* material with a smattering of new material, the overall tone being slightly less deep and introspective as *Wings*. But *You Never Walk Alone* was an indication that the Korean group most certainly had the Midas touch.

Preceding its February 14 release, *You Never Walk Alone* had already sold 700,000 copies. Spearheaded by the immediate singles success of 'Spring Day," "Not Today' and a very smart remake of "Outro: Wings" the album rocketed up the charts internationally, had a strong debut in America, debuting at No. 61 on the *Billboard Top 200 Album* Chart and quickly achieved platinum status with more than four million copies sold. BTS could conceivably do no wrong in the eyes of their adoring fans.

Once again it was time to pack their bags and hit the concert trail.

Chapter Fifteen
Can You Top This??

Speculation of an upcoming tour in support of *Wings* had been burning up the Internet. It intensified with the release of *You Never Walk Alone*. In November 2016, *BTS Live Episode III: The Wings Tour* was officially announced. It would be a world tour of mammoth proportions.

The *Wings Tour* ran from February 18, 2017 to December 10, 2017 and would encompass 40 shows in 19 cities. Bookended by stops in South Korea, the tour would also take in performances in Chile, Brazil, the United States, Thailand, Indonesia, The Philippines, Hong Kong, Australia, Japan, Taiwan and Macao. Not surprisingly, an estimated 550,000 tickets, taking in the entire tour, reportedly sold out within hours of the tour's announcement.

Far from being a "just the hits" performance, the Wings song list was designed to showcase the recent songs from *Wings* and *You Never Walk Alone* as well as prime moments from earlier albums. That in itself was a major undertaking. The show ran a fairly lengthy two and a half hours, showcased 23 songs, and was broken up by four intermissions and an encore. Technology remained a serious element of BTS*'s* performance with VCR images and the latest addition, seven solo stages for the individual members to strut their stuff during solo moments. Of course, there was the expected interplay between the group and audience, highlighted by the fact that, collectively, BTS had become quite fluent in English.

The excitement and expectations for this second world tour was palpable, as witness a group Q&A conducted by the *MSO* public relations firm prior to the start of the tour. RM teased the interviewer when asked about what fans could expect of the *Wings'* tour when he said, "I won't promise you anything fancy but I can tell you for sure there will be great songs and well-prepared performances." Jimin gleefully told the assembled media, "Whatever you expect from BTS, it's going to be better and more special." V was more specific. "Fans should look forward to active and fun interaction with BTS and an awesome performance on stage."

BTS was confident of their abilities to pull off a show that, on both technological and creative levels, was growing by leaps and bounds. In their minds, BTS saw the future as a place where anything was possible. But, in private moments, they acknowledged that the *Wings Tour* would tell them a lot

The two shows in South Korea that kicked off the *Wings Tour* were all that was promised and a whole lot more. While rarely straying far from the distinct notion of *BTS* as a living, breathing creative entity, the marathon concert was quick to draw a line between the idea of *BTS* as a cohesive group and the individual talents and identities of each member.

For those who were witnessing the group live for the first time, it was an extraordinary shock to their psyches. The band's combination of taut, personal messages wrapped around mainstream pop elements and choreography found BTS at a positive crossroads of their past and their future. The ease with which they interacted with the audience and turned the whole BTS experience into one big joyous party was a rousing success

After a final curtain call, the members of BTS left the stage to thunderous applause. They were tired and victorious. They had done their job. The triumph and the memories would last forever in the lives of their fans. The first stop on the *Wings* tour had proven a rousing success. The challenge would be to do it again in South America.

Chile and Brazil had always remained a happy mystery for the band, especially in Chile where mainstream commercial radio did not play BTS music. Sales of their previous albums had always been decent but did not provide a clue to how rabid and fanatic the fan support was that had grown around these seven South Korean boys. In a *New York Times* article, it was reported that a key to BTS's success in Chile had been twofold, the use of social media to get the word out and the influence of a K-Pop music program in the country that aired only once a week but had a respectable 40,000 listeners.

How BTS blew up in South America would become evident on the *Wings* tour when the four shows (March 11 and 12 in Santiago, Chile and March 19 and 20 in Sao Palo, Brazil) sold out literally in hours. That was expected.

What was not expected was a fan outrage that caused promoters to move one of the shows to a larger venue and raise the number of tickets sold to 60,000. The sudden impact of BTS mania in Chile became evident when a one of the country's major television stations broke into their regular programming for a live report on the arrival of BTS in their country. As reported by the *New York Times*, there was pandemonium in the airport when the plane landed and the group, surrounded by a massive entourage, disembarked and made their way through hundreds of screaming and banner-carrying fans. At one point a teary-eyed girl responded to a reporter's question of whether her wait had been worth it, by saying, "The wait! The whole night! Yes, it was worth it!"

With a couple of days off between the shows in Chile and Brazil, the group chose to maximize their exposure in the Spanish-speaking world by making a quick hop to Mexico and headlining the *Mexico K Con Convention*, an up and coming offshoot of the popular K Con Korean pop culture conventions. BTS's appearance was a success but would be marred by verbal clashes between their supporters and followers of another group on the bill. Hard feelings would eventually be smoothed over but it was a reminder that even the biggest K-Pop band in the world could still encounter overzealous fans and less than pleasant situations. Then it was back on a plane and back to Brazil to finish out their South American performances

Over a four night stay in Chile and Brazil, BTS rewarded the sold-out crowds with a mesmerizing series of shows, their lighting-like moves and tight sense of harmony and rapid fire rap and hip-hop stylings played out in a non-stop display of the impact of a new kind of music in a foreign land. BTS were in a truly emotional state as they concluded the last of their South American shows, telling the audience, as reported by *Korea Portal.com*, that "You are our wings and thanks to you, we are flying well.

"We look forward to sharing more laughing and crying moments."

Next stop America.

Chapter Sixteen
Okay by Me in America

By all accounts, the plane ride from Brazil to New Jersey in the United States was uneventful. Inside the cabin was dark and reportedly BTS and the other members of their entourage were in deep sleep. And who could blame them?

The South American portion of the *Wings Tour*, with the last-minute scheduling of their appearance at Mexico's *K Con*, had been particularly strenuous. The rehearsals, non-stop promotion and interviews and other aspects of the touring life, had begun to weigh on the group of young stars.

All they wanted was a few hours of quiet and to be alone with their thoughts before beginning the life of a pop star all over again. New Jersey would be a good first test to just how much progress had been made in their conquest of America.

Album sales told part of the story and social media and the Internet were the obvious spearheads in getting the BTS message out. But like all universal forms of expression, it all boiled down to language and whether fans brought up on English would get the nuances as spoken in Korean? The question was answered when at one point in their two-night stand in New Jersey, RM, as reported by the *Bucks County Courier Times* and *The Burlington County Times,* screamed out to his appreciative fans "Take a look around. BTS in the Prudential Center. Two shows sold out! Am I dreaming?"

BTS would make news even before the lights went down on the first New Jersey show when fans arriving for the concert were greeted by the Essex County Bomb Disposal Unit. The bomb squad had been summoned to the arena when a social media report warned that there would be a bomb at the BTS concert and, upon arrival, focused their attention on the BTS light sticks carried by the fans. But after ten minutes of inspecting the light sticks, it was determined that the warning had been a false alarm and the bomb squad left.

New Jersey reporters found their own answers as to what made BTS tick as they fanned out into the audience to put the question to concert goers. The Internet and social media were the answers they heard most often but there were also responses that went deeper into the soul of BTS and expression. A fan who had travelled all the way from Texas to New Jersey to see the show, summed those feelings up quite succinctly when she said "You don't need to understand the lyrics to feel the emotions of the song."

The New Jersey shows indicated that BTS had arrived as the consummate experience, music, songs, choreography, video and stage technology, not to mention the winning personalities of the group, combined for a concert experience that touched fans on any number of emotional and, yes, spiritual and philosophical levels.

A point driven home at the conclusion of the second Prudential Center show when RM once again addressed the crowd. "Music and performance transcends language, countries and race. I don't care if you're red, orange, green, purple or whatever. Thank you!"

RM remained effusive in his excitement over the New Jersey shows as reported by the *Orange County Register* when he exclaimed, "So many people just to see BTS was really an honor. It feels dreamy these days."

The next stop was the Allstate Arena in Chicago, yet another example of how BTS had taken over the hearts and minds of teenage America. The structure of the show continued at a mighty clip, proclaiming the hopes, dreams and potential for life that easily resonated with their young audience. At the conclusion of the Chicago show, RM and Jungkook stepped to the front of the stage and thanked the crowd. As reported in *NaverTV.com*, RM acknowledged the audience. "We are very excited to be back in the United States and impressed with your support and love." Jungkook chimed in with "I hope that you do not forget that we are always far away but we are together."

At that moment, RM took a good natured jab at his friend when he told the crowd, "You probably don't know this but he rehearsed that line a million times to get it right."

BTS moved on to Los Angeles for two concerts on April 1 and 2 at the Honda Center in Anaheim. By now, the routine of life on the road was quite predictable. Meeting with important people on the business side of the music scene, doing some fan related events and doing a seemingly endless array of interviews. BTS found the more teen-oriented and fan-friendly media events to be the easiest. Pose for group photos, answer fairly softball questions and crack jokes in the face of appreciative interviewers. The type of things pop culture celebrities had been doing seemingly forever.

But as the group became more popular, a more mature breed of journalists was now seemingly asking tougher and more thought-provoking questions. Such was the case when RM, who even at this stage was doing most of the one on one interviews, did a phone interview with a reporter for *The Orange County Register* newspaper. RM was well versed in most of the questions from the reporter and was ready with patented sound bite responses. But there was one that caused him to think a bit.

He was asked to contemplate the idea that BTS, like the Backstreet Boys, 'N'Sync and The Jonas Brother before them, might have a short life span before disbanding to go onto individual projects. RM did not think that would happen to BTS as the group already has side projects that did not interfere with their core group.

"I always tell them that every time we have hits under the name BTS, we shine the best when we are a team. I know all the seven members love music and I know their number one wish is for us to perform and make music and sing and dance. Maybe someday someone will want to be on a television show or be an actor. I just hope they know all of the popularity and fame and money is from the name of our team. That's not just one person. Everybody contributes to the team."

While in Los Angeles, BTS had yet another encounter with the dark side of the same social media that had helped propel them to the top. According to a report by the *Straits Times*, *Digital Music News* and other outlets, a negative Internet trolling campaign had emerged in recent months that indicated that BTS had been disrespectful to international fans and, with the group in Los Angeles, had morphed into a specific threat on the life of Jimin. The threats were not being taken seriously by Big Hit Entertainment who released a statement reported by *Soompi.com* and other outlets that said, "We believe it [the threats] are a joke by an anti-fan. But just to be sure we are taking measures. We are working with the local staff of the concert venue and police to enforce the security."

If the threats had any impact on BTS, it could not be judged by their performances at the Anaheim Honda Center on April 1 and 2. If anything, this being the final North American stop on the *Wings Tour* seemed to energize the group. For the group, the concert format was by this time very familiar. But they seemed encouraged by the idea of showcasing their talents in front of an audience that was seeing BTS 2017 for the first time. The entire set list seemed snappier, the vocals edgy in a slick K-Pop manner and the choreography easily on par with many a Broadway musical.

The give and take between BTS and the audience was palpable. When the screaming fans spontaneously began to sing along with the group, it was with a passion that defied any language and cultural barriers. Those who did not know a word of Korean were emotionally and spiritually intertwined with BTS. It was a sure sign of longevity for BTS and their fans. They would thrive and go into the future together.

RM could relate to this magic, career defining

moment. It was in a time and a place far removed from the first time they toured America. "We actually were scared of performing in America. I was really nervous. But after we were on stage, our fear disappeared. The fans are like everybody. They're like friends. Singing along through all of the lyrics even through the raps. They know how to play through the rhythms and the dances."

RM had predicted such a moment in their career, when everything just clicked, when he spoke to the *Orange County Register* in the days leading up to the Los Angeles concerts. "Nobody knows the future. I just hope that it can last as long as possible."

Chapter Seventeen
The Road Goes On

With the North American leg of the *Wings Tour* now over, BTS took a couple of weeks off before heading back to the other side of the world to begin what would an extensive Asian jaunt with stops in Thailand, Indonesia, The Philippines and China between April 22 and May 14. But the memories of the impact that BTS was having on the United States was still fresh in their minds as RM told the *Orange County Register* as the US portion of the Wings Tour was winding down.

"BTS music sounds like it's from America," he offered. "We decide to always watch the trends and watch what's going on over the world. America's the No. 1 market in the world so that's why people in America prefer us."

But having a foundation in US pop, R&B and rap has never been an impediment to the group gathering worldwide success and acceptance, the post North American *Wings Tour* early dates of Asia being a prime example. The shows were predictable in terms of the hysteria BTS brought wherever they performed. But what many observers believed was that the music itself was what made BTS something special beyond the teenage fan expectations. In execution, BTS is different from every other K-Pop group to this point. The novelty and bubblegum aspects of the genre have, with maturity, taken a backseat to the notion that K-Pop can be more adult and less disposable Throughout the Asia dates, there was a discernable sense of knowing and importance in the songs.

And as they would find out, by the time they took their final bow in Hong Kong, the important elements of the music business were beginning to sit up and take notice. The success of BTS on the *Billboard* charts had quickly become an ultimate goal for the group, the final frontier of acceptance. Which was why the members of BTS were thrilled when they received a call, telling them to hop on a plane and fly back to the states, specifically Las Vegas, Nevada, for what would turn out to be a very special moment.

The Billboard Music Awards was an important step up the ladder of success. It was a chance to be seen with some of the biggest names in popular music and the awards given would be a barometer of an artist's standing in the industry. Those were the thoughts flashing through the minds of the BTS members as they walked the proverbial red carpet into the auditorium where the ceremony would be held. The screaming fans who had made the pilgrimage to Las Vegas to cheer them on was heartwarming and the opportunity to mix and mingle with the likes of Justin Bieber, Selena Gomez, Ariana Grande and Shawn Mendes and be true fans quite literally brought BTS back to their roots.

But those moments would be anti-climactic to the moment in the awards show when it was announced that BTS was named the winner of the *Top Social Artist Award* for 2017. The significance of the group being the first K-Pop band to win a *Billboard Music Award* was not lost on the group. As reported by *CNN* and countless other media outlets, BTS stood at center stage, accepted the honor with grace and RM addressed the audience.

"We still cannot believe that we are standing on this stage at the *Billboard Music Awards*. It's so great to see all the artists we admire and we feel honored to be in this category, with all these great artists in front of us."

BTS barely had time to deal with the post *BMA* accolades when they were back on the road for the second half of their *Wings Tour*. The May 26 show in Australia was a reminder that the group was easily expanding their creative empire around the world. The tour continued with a May 30-July 2 blitz of Japan which brought the *Wings Tour* to its official conclusion. BTS were jubilant in thanking the audience after the final show as reported by *The Korea Herald*. "We would like to thank our fans across the world. This honor belongs to all of you!"

But the life of a by now world-famous pop group always seemed to be balanced out by real world hard work. Right in the middle of the *Wings Tour*, at the conclusion of the Japan shows, Big Hit Entertainment announced that the group had evolved into a new brand and identity with a brand new logo and the alternative English language name of Beyond The Scene. Many observers of the scene took this enhanced image as a sign that BTS would soon be resting on their laurels and heading in a more commercial direction.

As it turned out, nothing could be further from the truth.

By September, BTS's legion of fans would know, with the release of the nine-song EP entitled *Love Yourself: Her* that the group was turning a very important creative page. In conception, *Love Yourself: Her* presented itself as more of a hip-hop album than previous efforts, with an emphasis on electro pop and dance sounds. Lyrically such songs as "Go Go" and "DNA" came across as personal observations and journal entries.

But in a conversation with *Billboard*, RM explained how the songs on the album had taken a much more reflective turn and were, creatively, a first for the group and a definite part of a growth process within BTS. "The songs on this album are completely personal and relatable. "DNA" is the expression of young, passionate love. "Go Go" is about how young people are living their lives with little money and low expectations in their lives. The songs on this album are taking us to new ground. We tried to apply new grammar and new perspectives, technically and musically it is very different from what we've done before. This album is the starting point of a second chapter of our career."

And it was a new chapter that, for the first time, featured BTS working in collaboration with an outside musician. At the BMA's, the band met with the American electronic pop duo The Chainsmokers. They clicked as friends with the same musical vibe and, during the recording of *Love Yourself: Her*, Chainsmoker member Andrew Taggert submitted some beats and samples that ultimately resulted in Taggert co-writing the song "Best of Me" with RM, Suga and J-Hope. It was a break-through moment that indicated that BTS had become comfortable with

America's music consciousness and was willing to collaborate with other musicians.

Pre-release promotion for *Love Yourself: Her* hit the Internet in waves beginning in early August as a literal tidal wave of posters, photos, teaser trailers and song clips which, in turn, led to an unbelievable rollout of interest and sales. Between August 25 and 31, Big Hit Entertainment and its regional distributors totaled more than a million pre-sale orders. September 18 saw the simultaneous release of *Love Yourself: Her* and the music video of the first single "DNA." The album sold more than a million copies in less than a month while the video was viewed 21 million times in 24 hours. The album debuted at No. 1 on the Korean charts. "DNA" debuted at No. 2 on the Korean Singles chart. All nine tracks on *Love Yourself: Her* appeared on the Top 40 Korean Digital Charts. Continuing their conquest of America, the album debuted at No. 7 on the *Billboard Top 200* album charts. Quite simply, *Love Yourself Her* was BTS's crowning achievement to that point, one that would make the top of the charts in 73 different countries and stay there well into the New Year.

RM reflected on the success *of Love Yourself: Her* when he told *CNN,* "The success is amazing to us. We really started at the bottom. When we first started, no one paid any attention to us." But he also indicated that the universal appeal of the new album could not be denied. "The new album is all about closing barriers, language, borders and connecting with the human experience. Our songs are about the hardships of young people, their loves and their daily lives."

Nearly lost in the rush to praise the album as a whole was a highly experimental collaboration between BTS and producer/performer Steve Aoki and US rapper Designer on the remix of the song 'Mic Drop.' Working with established stars outside the BTS realm was one thing. Doing the song in English rather than Korean was a whole different turn, a sign of creative progress as well as a nod to the reality of the business.

RM explained in a conversation with the fan translation channel *Bangtan Subs* that reaching a larger audience with 'Mic Drop,'' "We rewrote the lyrics in English for the song to be able to be heard by more people. This is our first time attempting to do this so I can't imagine how this will turn out."

How "Mic Drop" turned out was amazing. The song peaked at No. 23 on the Korea charts but where it made its real impact was in America. "Mic Drop" peaked at No. 28 on the *Billboard Hot 100* chart, the first time a K-Pop song cracked that coveted listing.

BTS had become the feel-good story of the year and their growing influence on a worldwide scale had not gone unnoticed by the music industry. And so, it was with no small amount of fanfare that the announcement came in early November that the group had been invited to be one of the featured performers at that year's prestigious *American Music Awards*, November 19, in Los Angeles.

The international flight carrying BTS touched down in Los Angeles International Airport. Inside the young men looked out their windows as their plane glided to a stop. By now, they knew what would come next. The screaming fans, the paparazzi, cries of admiration and love for their favorite group member as they moved inside a cocoon of security through the airport and out into the day. But inside, the thoughts were more personal. They were tired from the long flight, they had a weeks' worth of glad handing the press and an endless number of radio and television personalities to deal with. It would be fun but it would also be hard work.

And then there was that little matter of making history as the first ever K-Pop group to perform live at the *American Music Awards*. This was important, a lingering memory that would last, and that would be proof positive that they had finally arrived at the pinnacle of stardom.

The following week was a blur of activity. Appearances on radio and television outlets, the likes of *On Air with Ryan Seacrest*, *Jimmy Kimmel Live* and *The Late Late Show with James Cordon* were awash in softball questions, joking bits and pithy anecdotes from the group that had already been heard countless times before, flew by in a haze of glitz and hype. The only relevant question centered around how it felt to be the first K-Pop group to perform live at the *American Music Awards*? And for that BTS did not have a question.

At least not yet.

That answer would come on Sunday, November 19. The group had already gone through a rehearsal. The sound was just right for what they hoped would be an electrifying live version of "DNA." Later that evening, the group was driven to the Microsoft Theater. They were excited and there was a sense of anticipation in the air. As they walked down the red carpet in front of the cameras and the fans who screamed and yelled out the names of their favorite,

BTS was blown away by the recognition and the adulation. They had heard it before and their reaction remained the same.

"Screaming crowds still surprise us," RM told *E News.com*. "It is like something that we can never get used to. It is new every day."

Hours later, BTS were shifting uneasily backstage as they awaited the announcement that would bring them to the stage for their big moment. RM admitted later that the group was so nervous that they could hardly look beyond the stage. "We were so nervous that we couldn't even watch the audience."

BTS hit the stage to thunderous applause. The stage fright disappeared instantly, replaced by a sonic boom of music, choreography and lightning moves amid a cacophony of lyrical and vocal energy. The audience threw all notions of business cool aside and were immediately on their feet, dancing and waving their fists in the air. "DNA" finished with a flourish of emotion and accomplishment. BTS smiled amid sustained applause from the music veterans and moguls. They had brought people to their feet in a rush of youthful exuberance.

Backstage, BTS was all smiles. They were mentally and physically exhausted. But in the eyes of their peers, they were triumphant. RM, who was rarely at a loss for words, seemed particularly overwhelmed by their performance. When asked by the gathering media how it felt, all he could manage was…

"Our performance was sick."

Chapter Eighteen
Next Stop: 2018

It was doubtful anyone would have noticed if BTS had taken a few weeks off following their victory lap at the *American Music Awards*. But sitting back and resting on their laurels was not the way BTS rolled.

They would return to their roots in a very expansive way between December 8th and 10th, when they closed out their formal concert year with three sold-out shows at the South Korea Gocheok Sky Dome in front of an estimated 60,000 fans. Two days after the final show, BTS announced that they had the singular honor of performing at the annual *Dick Clark's New Year's Rockin' Eve 2018*. A statement from the band indicated, "We are honored to celebrate this amazing year and to ring in this amazing year by performing."

Into 2018, BTS sat back and watched as the awards rolled in. Japan had proven a potent sales magnet with over 500,000 copies of their triple A side single "Mic Drop/DNA/Crystal Snow/" resulting in a double platinum certification in January. That same month, BTS added the *Golden Disc Award* and the *Seoul Music Awards* to their never-ending string of accomplishments. February brought the first acknowledgement of the New Year in America when the singles "Mic Drop Remix" and "DNA" were both certified gold.

No new product from BTS was scheduled in March but that did not stop the group from, singularly and collectively, from satisfying their fans. An eight hour documentary of their just completed *Wings* tour, entitled *Burn the Stage*, which chronicled both the onstage life and behind the scenes antics of the super group on the road, was released to YouTube. But, perhaps most important to the creative life of BTS, came with the March release of J-Hope's debut mixed tape entitled *Hope World*.

Hope World was a tough but ruggedly individual look at J-Hope's world, a two-year odyssey of creating, piecemeal, an album during recordings in hotel rooms and in other private moments on tours and away from group activities. And it would be well worth the wait. Alternatively, observant and confessional, *Hope World* borrowed from divergent influences such as science fiction writer Jules Verne and his personal observations on life and the challenges and the price one paid for celebrity and success, all done up in an enticing mix of pop, rap and exotic tropical beats.

In conversation with *Time Magazine*, J-Hope acknowledged the often challenging odyssey to creating *Hope World*. "The team always comes first so I focused on our projects as BTS and tried to make time whenever I could to create my calling card to the world. RM and Suga releasing their own mixtapes was the motivation for my own project. I started dancing first but I also felt I could tell my story through my music. I wanted to put my own story to music and share it with the world."

Hope World was an immediate success and teased

fans for what they hoped would be the next BTS album. In difference to their legions of fans in Japan, BTS released their third Japanese language album entitled *Face Yourself* on April 4. This 12-track album featured eight Japanese language versions of songs from their previous albums *Wings* and *Love Yourself: Her*, was a huge success and, perhaps, a bit of a surprise. Not a whole lot of promotion had been put into the release but *Face Yourself* debuted at No. 43 on the *Billboard Top 200* album chart and became the first Japanese album to be certified Platinum in that country. But fans were getting antsy and the Internet was a live with questions of what would come next.

They would not have long to speculate when, on April 16, BTS announced the particulars of their new music with a flourish and a bit of mystery. The flourish was a nine-minute long video entitled *Euphoria: Theme of Love Yourself and Wonder*, which included the expected new single, "Euphoria," sung by Jungkook. Replete with strong tropical beats, glossy metaphysical style imagery and a stirring sense of introspection, the consensus was that this was the unveiling of the long speculated theory of the next album in *Love Yourself* series being *Love Yourself: Wonder*, a seemingly esoteric left turn that would, reportedly, focus on Korean literary terms and storytelling techniques. It would be speculation that would quickly be denied.

When the truth was revealed, the next album, entitled *Love Yourself: Tear*, with a scheduled May 18 release date, was an ambitious thematic collection whose 11 songs focused on the pain and suffering of love and separation. Going into production, *Love Yourself: Tear* was being touted as a deeply personal album and, according to a joint group statement in *Soompi.com*, nobody took the album more personally than RM. "RM had a hand in the entire album creation process. We even saw him staying up all night writing lyrics for V. He was so excited and was saying to himself 'I'm sure V is going to like this.'"

By now, even more highbrow journalists, who tended to dismiss BTS as a pre-fab pop group in the past, had begun to take *Love Yourself: Tear* with a bit more respect and their interviews with BTS on the promotion tour began to delve deeper into feelings behind the current batch of songs. And more often than not, it would fall to RM to field the more serious questions from the likes of *Billboard* and *EOnline.com* about the deep thoughts behind the songs.

"We're trying to say that, if you love, when you're not true to yourself, the love won't last because love is complex and we always have the dark sides and the bad sides. This time around it's about honesty and love. Sometimes we just turn away from some sorts of situations because, in love and life, it's not like a fairytale. We always have a dark side so we want to talk about the dark side."

But the question finally remained, would even an album by BTS finally cross the line of the most basic K-Pop criterion which was to keep things light, positive and danceable be commercial poison? As the days counted down to May 18, a whole lot of people silently said a prayer that the gods of K-Pop would continue to smile.

The group continued to press hype with a quick hop across the world to make a second visit to *The Ellen DeGeneres Show* where they performed the album's first single "Fake Love" and a live concert from Los Angeles which was broadcast around the world and featured several songs from *Love Yourself: Tear*. By that time, *Love Yourself: Tear* was already well on the way to be the biggest hit that BTS ever had.

Between April 18 and 25, advance orders for *Love Yourself: Tear* had already topped one and a half million copies. Following the official May 18 release, the album sold an additional two million copies in the space of two weeks. Once again, BTS*'s* incursion into America's psyche was the icing on the cake when *Love Yourself: Tear* debuted at No. 1 on the *Billboard Top 200* album charts. Throw in record sales in the UK, Japan and countless other countries and the reviews that indicated that BTS had now left their creative childhood behind and were now grown men and you had a scenario that was just too good to be true.

While collectively thrilled at the album's success, RM remained reflective in the face of it all when he spoke to *Billboard*. "We're trying to enjoy the ride and trying to live in the moment," he offered. "If we set too many long term goals for ourselves, it just makes us tired."

By June 2018, the BTS odyssey was continuing nonstop down the tracks. And there was seemingly no end in sight."

Chapter Nineteen
Consider the Options

Or was there?

Lost amid the hype and hysteria of the *Love Yourself* Tour had been the possibility that this might well be the last BTS tour...or at least BTS in its current configuration. Because the specter of big business and big money was lurking in the background.

And the fact was that the contractual agreement between the members of BTS and Big Hit Entertainment would soon expire. The reality was that Big Hit Entertainment had recruited the members and molded them into the persona of BTS. The company had been extremely generous financially and had allowed them the creative freedom in solo efforts, producing and writing. And it went without saying that a basic trust in their respective instincts between Bang Si-hyuk and the individual members of the group had allowed BTS to expand far beyond the expectations of K-Pop.

But it was those self-same elements that had, in turn, made BTS a recognizable and beloved icon to countless millions of fans and, by association, had made the individual members stars in their own right. There had always been internet chatter, usually around the time of a solo release by a BTS member that somebody

109

was getting ready to leave the group for greener pastures. During those moments there would be speculation that one or more members could easily be replaced without losing the impact of the group identity.

And so, during the early stages of the *Love Yourself* tour, behind the scenes negotiations were going on between BTS and Big Hit Entertainment to either come to a happy ending or to begin laying the groundwork for BTS's future. The intensity of those negotiations and the terms of any potential agreement were never discussed publicly. For the fans it was all bright lights and good vibrations. It all remained to be seen.

On October 17, 2018, *Billboard*, *Hollywood Life* and countless other BTS-friendly media outlets would happily announce the news that BTS and Big Hit Entertainment had agreed to a new seven-year contract that would keep BTS in the Big Hit Entertainment fold until 2026.

A company statement was released. "It is our philosophy that we should cater the best to artists who are achieving unprecedented global success. After a thorough discussion with the seven members of BTS we decided to renew their contract before the world tour to ensure more stable, long term activities."

Also made public was a statement from BTS. "We respect our mentor and producer Bang Si-hyuk who has continued to show us a vision for our future even before our debut and has helped us form our perspective of the world and music. With Big Hit Entertainment's support, we will continue to strive to give our best to fans around the world."

It would not be long before news of the new contract spread around the world with the legions of BTS fans joyous at the news. One tweet from a fan was particularly telling. "Seriously guys, this is the best news ever! Another seven years with the seven boys who have made me the happiest."

Chapter Twenty
More, More, More

It seemed to many observers that Big Hit Entertainment and *BTS* had been stockpiling music for a long time, at least when it came to the dizzying speed in which new albums were being announced with surprising regularity, even by K-Pop standards. Such was definitely the case when on July 17, less than two months after *Love Yourself: Tear* became BTS's landmark release on the waves of critical and universal acceptance, their label was making the announcement that yet another album, *Love Yourself: Answer,* would be released on August 24.

On the surface, *Love Yourself: Answer* was a familiar format, a compilation album of 26 songs from the albums *Love Yourself: Her* and *Love Yourself: Tear* along with assorted remixes. But Love *Yourself: Answer* would have deeper ambitions.

Seven new songs were part of the package and were intended as an emotional connection and conclusion to the *Love Yourself* storyline. Thematically, such new songs as "Idol," "Fake Love" and "The Truth Untold" formed a solid emotional core, addressing the subjects of empowerment, youth, love and reflection in a way that linked the past and the present. The moods of the new material were powerful and deep, the notion of confidence, passion and yearning. Yes this was K-Pop and the tracks moved along on familiar riffs of BTS musical and lyrical notions. But even those predictable elements were mixed with new and enticing African and South Korean stylings. At the end of the day, *Love Yourself: Answer* would bring a satisfying ending to easily the most ambitious period in BTS's career.

While BTS's *Love Yourself* concept was wildly laudable, there was concern about how well the concept would fare over the life of three albums in a notoriously fickle music business in which styles and ambitious ideas faded in and out with regularity.

In a 2018, a Los Angeles press conference reported by *ET* and others, BTS addressed the idea of a three album arc. RM admitted, "Spreading the *Love Yourself* concept over three albums was a risky move. But we took the risk and so far it seems to have paid off." Jungkook added, "The *Love Yourself* concept shows us where we are and makes us think about our responsibilities to ourselves and to our fans in the music that we're making."

It did not take long for the public to validate *BTS's Love Yourself* crusade. In the days leading up to the official release of *Love Yourself: Answer*, preorders totaled nearly two million copies. The album debuted at No. 1 on *Korea's Gaon Album Chart*. Eight days into its official release and *Love Yourself: Answer* had already accounted for an additional two million copies sold. Not surprisingly, the album, spearheaded by first single "Idol" and a follow-up digital alternative version featuring vocals by Nicki Minaj, made its debut at No. 1 on the *Billboard Top 200* album chart.

But by the time *Love Yourself: Answer* was flirting with multi-platinum status, the BTS legions were already salivating at even bigger news. That BTS was getting ready to head out on their third world tour. On April 26, well ahead of the release of the album *Love Yourself: Tear*, Big Hit Entertainment had released an Internet trailer that announced that *BTS World Tour: Love Yourself* would begin on August 26.

BTS World Tour: Love Yourself would, in inception be a massive undertaking, taking in 12 countries including Japan, The United States, Canada, the United Kingdom, France, The Netherlands, Germany, Taiwan, Hong Kong, Singapore and Thailand, and would consist of 22 performances that would stretch out through the remainder of 2018 and into April 2019. The response from fans was instantaneous and unbelievable.

Tickets for the two Seoul, South Korea shows, a total of 90,000 tickets, went on sale April 4 and were sold out in a matter of seconds. When tickets for the Newark, Fort Worth and Los Angeles shows on the North American leg of the tour sold out in seconds on May 5, a second Los Angeles show was added to keep up with demand and it also sold out immediately. The remainder of the Canadian and US tour stops followed suit, as did the venues in Germany and The United Kingdom. Along the way, BTS would make history of sorts when the addition of a sports stadium in New York made the group the first K-Pop group to ever headline an outdoor stadium in the United States.

By the time *BTS* hit the road for the first stop on the *BTS World Tour: Love Yourself*, all 790,000 available tickets had been sold.

Rain was coming down in torrents on the first day of the *Love Yourself* tour at Seoul's famed Olympic Stadium. Mere hours before BTS hit the stage, the outdoor venue was a quagmire of mud and rain-soaked seats. It was not a good omen for what would be a very long tour. But then the weather gods had other ideas. The downpour suddenly turned to a drizzle. Literally moments before the concert was to start, the rain stopped all together. The conditions were not ideal, especially for the fans, but the show would go on.

"I think fortune was with us this day," Jin told *The Korea Herald.* "Today there was more than 80 percent chance of rain. But it didn't rain at all during our performance."

It was a performance that would be equal parts nostalgia and a trip down memory lane for *BTS* and their loyal fans. The set list seemingly touched on every aspect of their career with a large emphasis on the *Love Yourself* songs. Lyrically and musically the band was in top form, the elements of rap and hip hop taking on an extra amount of density and power against the backdrop of darkness and bad weather. It was BTS *i*n all their glory and the fans' response was electric in the face of the cold and damp conditions.

Jimin waxed nostalgic after that first performance when he told *The Korean Herald,* "This is our first time performing at Olympic Stadium and I missed the [Korean] fans so bad. I couldn't concentrate on stage as I was so awed by them. After performing 'Idol' I felt so tired but I also felt so great. I'm not lying. This moment will be the best I've had this year."

But as they moved to Los Angeles for the four-night stand on the North American leg of the tour,

BTS had seemed to have grown into their performance. That first night in Los Angeles, there were moments when the band seemed to be testing the perception of K-Pop male sexuality with choreographed moves that made them more human and comfortable with the changing world around them. While a group concept, *BTS* was showing moments of individual identities within the group and the promise of expanding the preconceived group concept. To be sure, the expected lyrical, musical and messages, combined with the choreography and visual stage magic, were by this time vintage BTS. But beyond the expectedness of it all, there were signs that BTS, during their Los Angeles shows, were growing into something much more expansive and promising than even they could have predicted.

During their stay in Los Angeles, representatives of The Grammy Museum interviewed BTS and the wide ranging Q&A touched on how the group was inspired and influenced creatively by their fans.

V said, "The fans gave us wings that allowed us to be where we are now. So, we are always thankful." Jungkook offered that the group felt they had a duty to their fans to do the best they can. "Success makes us think more about our responsibilities. How we should act. How we should make our music. So, it makes us think more deeply about what we do and how responsible we should be about what we're doing and the music we're making."

Throughout the remainder of the US portion of the tour, the response to BTS remained predictable in a positive way. The fans camping out for days around the venue, the unbridled enthusiasm and the rave reviews from the press. But when reporters in places like Oakland, Ca. and Fort Worth, Texas probed a bit deeper into the psyche of the fans, an interesting clue emerged to the effect that BTS was having. A large percentage of fans had traveled long distances to the show in areas where BTS music would not necessarily have a strong hold on music lovers. One enterprising reporter from *NBC5* in Fort Worth gathered some interesting emotional insights from a fan who had traveled all the way from New York to see the Texas show.

"I want to be the first person in general admission," ticked off Lexi Savetta in an almost mantra like manner. "I want to be the first person. I want to have the spot I want on the barricade. I don't know Korean. I don't understand it. But I like to listen to the music. It makes me feel good."

The fan frenzy and unabashed good vibes from the group followed BTS through stops in Canada, Newark and Chicago. Critics were falling all over themselves with breathless raves, extoling the BTS experience as something bigger than a mere pop music concert, rather a sonic and multicultural experience that was suddenly larger than life itself. This was a point that would be driven home in the last stop on the Northern leg of the tour, New York's Citi Field.

Big concerts in New York have always gone hand in hand. Back before a lot of you were born, The Beatles played Shea Stadium, the legendary Summer Jam took place in Watkins Glen, John Lennon played Madison Square Garden and, of course, there was that little get together called Woodstock. BTS's October 6 show at Citifield carried that same kind of vibe.

Excitement was in the air. If you listened closely to the thousands of fans who had camped out for a week prior to the show, you probably would have heard the words 'peace' and 'love' tossed around in hopeful tones.

The history of New York and large musical gatherings was not lost on the members of BTS. The anticipation level was high. For the group, there was a sense of history in the air. They group would most certainly pull out all the stops.

By now the set list and the show itself was fairly pat. Certain songs and emotional moments would go off on schedule. But this night in New York City, there was a sense of urgency and giving in the performance. The bond between BTS and the audience was wound extremely tight. BTS was giving it their all and the audience of 40,000 was returning the favor.

At the conclusion of the evening's final song, as reported by *Rolling Stone*, BTS stood at center stage, dripping sweat from their performance and emotionally drained as they took their bows. Jimin was visibly shaken and broke down in tears. It would remain for RM to express the group's emotions and appreciation.

"New York is the place where the music that changed my life was born. We are honored to be the first Korean musicians to play in a US stadium. It's never intended but I feel like I'm using you guys to love myself. Please use me."

Chapter Twenty-One
Winter Influence

In September 2018, RM stepped to the podium in front of a gathering of United Nations' dignitaries from around the world. Being in front of crowds was not something new. But being in front of the United Nations, well this was a whole different story. BTS*'s* longstanding dedication to dealing with the challenges and issues of young people in their music had put the group in the forefront of worldwide issues pertaining to children. BTS was in New York to help launch a worldwide initiative called *Generation Unlimited* that had been conceived to bring global opportunities to the younger generation, as reported by *The Washington Post*, *Billboard* and other media outlets.

In a heartfelt speech before the UN, RM reflected on his growing up in South Korea, the challenges he faced growing up and how BTS had come to reflect the issues being faced by their fans while often struggling with their own personal and human issues. RM would end his speech by encouraging the young people to step up and let their voices be heard.

"Those stories we hear from fans constantly remind us of our responsibility. Let's all take one more step. We have learned to love ourselves so I urge you

119

to speak yourself. No matter who you are, where you're from, your skin color or gender identity, speak yourself. Find your name. Find your voice by speaking yourself."

With this speech, *BTS* had suddenly found itself transformed from pop music superstars to legitimate leaders in a growing movement to empower the current generation of youth and the generations that would follow. The sudden rush of notoriety from the UN speech would soon find BTS on the cover of the international edition of *Time Magazine* in an issue titled Next Generation Leaders that featured up and coming young leaders in different strata of society. BTS was selected on the basis of one of the most popular acts of their generation as well as their steadfast loyalty to their home country of South Korea. On this occasion, RM told *Billboard,* "As a Korean, we love our country and we're proud of our country. It's just an honor to be called an ambassador of Korean K-Pop."

Shortly after the *Time Magazine* announcement, RM surprised the legions of fans with some creative news. Three days before its release, it was announced that RM's second solo release, a seven-song collection entitled *Mono* would be available. For the young rapper, *Mono* would be considered a radical departure. The seven songs were sung in both Korean and English and the tone of the collection was highly introspective with a sense of world weariness and loneliness weaving in and out of the softer, more exotic instrumentation and contemplative lyrics.

Late in the year, BTS broke new ground with the release of *Burn the Stage: The Movie*, a documentary of life on the road. The film was released directly to theaters and opened in mid-November to a crowd primed and ready for yet more BTS. That *Burn the Stage: The Movie* would prove to be an instant commercial success did not surprise. By early December the BTS concert movie had garnered the biggest-ever box office haul for an event cinema release raking in $18.5 million around the world, according to *Variety*.

BTS had long since returned to the *Love Yourself* tour, burning through the European leg with sold-out concerts in the United Kingdom, The Netherlands, Germany and France through the month of October and the Asia leg (Japan, Singapore and Hong Kong) well into December. At this point, the BTS experience had evolved from mere spectacle to something much more deep and intimate. There was the excitement and the bombast to be sure. But most importantly there was a connection between BTS and its fans, a bond once forged that could not be broken. BTS had, on the wings of massive adulation, broken through to something more important.

It appeared that by the end of 2018, BTS had captured just about every nomination and award the music industry had to offer. But as the group prepared their lives for the activities of Christmas and New Year. They would be recognized one more time. On December 7, it was announced that BTS would make history when the news broke that they would become the first K-Pop act in history to be nominated for a Grammy Award. Although the nomination would be in the category of *Best Recording Package* and had nothing to do with their music, BTS was not

121

disappointed. The nomination was just another proof to the growing list of evidence that BTS had truly arrived.

BTS was now the moniker of a universal language that spoke of one thing... Love.

Chapter Twenty-Two
What's Next?

If you've gotten this far, the answer to the question of 'What's next?' is open to conjecture. For BTS what's next is this. The seemingly never-ending *Love Yourself* tour is booked solid until late April 2019. Barring any last minute additional shows, that's when the tour will officially end.

Beyond that is anybody's guess.

As of this writing, no new music is scheduled to be released. But this being K-Pop and the prolific BTS, I would be cautious on betting against another album in the first quarter of 2019. Reports indicate that BTS, collectively and as solo artists, have a lot of songs ready to be released, more than enough to keep the BTS fans in K-Pop heaven. The status of the band as a unit, despite the inevitable Internet rumblings, would seem to be set in the wake of their recent contract extension. Long story short, BTS is primed to stay intact for years to come.

But owing to South Korea's stringent laws about celebrities having to serve time in the military, that could change. Word along the BTS grapevine is that at least four of the seven members could be required to do some form of military service during the life of their current contract. But at this point, it's all speculation, rumor and conjecture.

There is also evidence in the K-Pop industry that more groups will begin to follow the blueprint of BTS. There is already talk that Big Hit Entertainment will be unveiling a new group, a five piece, very young boy band that will be very much in the mold of their older brothers.

As for the group itself? Two thousand nineteen might just be the time to sit back and relax. Nobody is going to argue that the group doesn't deserve some time off. This year might be the time to reflect, do a solo project or work with other musicians, be with their family, have relationships and essentially deal with the real world before returning to the fantasy that is BTS.

One thing is certain however.

As the coming years play out, BTS will have already secured a place in pop music history. They are true international stars. But perhaps most important is the fact that they've opened up a whole new world of K-Pop, one with endless creative possibilities that transcend the predictable and disposable nature of the music and the art form and turned it into something that will finally emerge as a legacy that is legitimate and long lasting.

There's a sign post up ahead, pointing toward endless possibilities. And BTS will most certainly be leading the way.

BTS looking too cool in black and white at the 32nd Annual Golden Awards. How long do you think they can hold that pose? *(Photo courtesy of Wiki Commons)*

BTS strikes a thinking man's pose during a 2018 photo shoot for an electronics ad. Deep thoughts for certain. *(Photo courtesy of Wiki Commons)*

BTS in a dream state, contemplating the girl of their dream during a photo shoot for a cellphone ad. Is the girl you? *(Photo courtesy of Wiki Commons)*

All smiles as they accept yet another award at the 31st Golden Disc Awards in Seoul, South Korea. BTS could get used to this. And they have. *(Photos courtesy of Wiki Commons)*

Lights! Camera! BTS! And the crowd goes wild during a 2014 M.Net Countdown show. *(Photo courtesy of Wiki Commons)*

BTS's moves can't be beat during an electrifying moment of song and dance during the 2016 YouTube Fan Fest performance in South Korea. *(Photo courtesy of Wiki Commons)*

Showcasing slick choreography and cool moves during a 2016 press conference for The Most Beautiful Moment In Life on Stage Tour. *(Photo courtesy of Wiki Commons)*

The highlight of any BTS show is when J-Hope takes center stage and sings about being in the mood for love during a 2016 show in Taipei. *(Photo courtesy of Wiki Commons)*

APPENDIX
Discography

Singles

Lists all known released singles, albums and EP's through 2018 but does not take into account high or low chart positions.

Korean

2013
No More Dream, We Are Bulletproof, Part II, NO, I like It, Satori Pop, Attack of Bangtan, We, On

2014
Boy In Luv, Just One Day, Danger, War of Hormone, If I Ruled The World, Where You From?, Tomorrow, Jump, Spine Breaker, Cypher Part 2: Triptych, Outro Propose, Skool Luv Affair, Soulmate, Miss Right, Rain, Blanket Kick, Let Me Know, Heaven, Look Here, Would You Turn Off Your Cellphone?, Second Grade, Hip Hop Lover, Killer, What Am I To You?, Does That Make Sense? What Are You Doing?

2015
I Need U, Dope, Run, Hold Me Tight, Converse High, Boyz With Fun, Love is Not Over, Moving On, The

Most Beautiful Moment in Life, Expectation,
Butterfly, Whalien 52, Autumn Leaves, Ma City,
Silver Spoon/Crow Tilt, House of Cards, Never Mind,
One Night in a Strange City

2016
Epilogue: Young Forever, Fire, Save Me, Blood Sweat
& Tears, Butterfly, Love Is Not Over, House of Cards,
Run, I Need You, Lie, Stigma, Begin, Lost, 21st
Century Girls, Awake, First Love, Still Wishing There
Will Be Better Days, Am I Wrong?, Mama,
Reflection, Boy Meets Evil, Wings

2017
Spring Day, Not Today, DNA, You Never Walk
Alone, Outro Wings, Best of Me, Dimple, Pied Piper,
Go Go Go, Mic Drop, Serendipity, Outro Her,

2018
Fake Love, Idol, The Truth Untold, 134340, Paradise,
Love Maze, Magic Shop, Anpanman, Airplane Part 2,
So What? Singularity, Outro Tear, Euphoria, I'm Fine,
Love Myself, Epiphany, Just Dance, Seesaw, Love,
Serendipity

Japanese

2014
No More Dream, Boy in Love, Danger

2015
For You, I Need U

2016
Run

2017
Crystal Snow, Mic Drop/DNA/Crystal Snow

2018
Fake Love/Airplane Part 2, Let Go, Ringwandering,
Crack

English

2017
Mic Drop

2018
Euphoria, I'm Fine, Love Myself, Epiphany, Just
Dance, Seesaw, Love, Serendipity, Idol

Albums
This list includes all albums in all formats and
encompasses releases in all countries

2013
2 Kool 4 Skool, O!RUL8.2?

2014
*Dark and Wild, Skool Luv Affair, Skool Luv Affair:
Special Edition*

2015
*The Most Beautiful Moment in Life, Part 1, The Most
Beautiful Moment in Life, Part 2*

2016
Wings, The Most Beautiful Moment in Life: Young Forever

2017
You Never Walk Alone, Love Yourself: Her

2018
Love Yourself: Tear, Love Yourself: Answer

Music Videos

2013
No More Dream, No More Dream (Dance Version), *We Are Bulletproof, Part 2, No*

2014
Boy in Luv, Boy in Luv (Dance Version), *Just One Day, Just One Day* (Dance Version), *Just One Day* (Facial Expression Version), *Just One Day* (One Take Version), *No More Dream* (Japanese Version), *Boy in Luv* (Japanese Version), *Danger, War of Hormone, Danger* (Japanese Version)

2015
I Need U, I Need U (Original Version), *For You, For You* (Dance Version), *Dope, Run, I Need U* (Japanese Version)

2016
Run (Japanese Version), *Epilogue: Young Forever, Fire, Fire* (Dance Version), *Save Me, August D, Give It to Me, Blood Sweat & Tears*

2017
Spring Day, *Not Today*, *Not Today* (Choreography Version), *Blood Sweat & Tears* (Japanese Version), *Come Back Home*, *DNA*, *Mic Drop* (Steve Aoki Remix), *Mic Drop* (Japanese Version/Short Version), *With Soul*

2018
Fake Love, *Fake Love* (Extended Version), *Idol*, *Idol* (featuring Nicki Minaj), *Airplane Part 2* (Japanese Version)

International Awards
(Wins and nominations noted)

Billboard Music Awards
2017: Top Social Artist (Won)
2018: Favorite Social Artist (Won) Top Social Artist (Won)

BBC Radio One Teen Awards
2018: Best International Group (Won) Best Social Media Star (Won)

Break Tudo Awards (Brazil)
2017: Best International Group (Won) Best Fandom (Won)
2018: Best International Group (Won) Best K-Pop Male Group (Won) Best Fandom (Won)

E People's Choice Awards
2018: Group of The Year (Won) Social Celebrity of The Year (Won) Song of The Year (Idol) (Won) Music Video of the Year (Idol) (Won)

MTV Europe Awards
2014: Best Korean Act (Nominated)
2015: Best Korean Act (Won) Biggest Worldwide Act
(Asia) (Nominated)
2018: Biggest Fans (Won) Biggest Group (Won)

MTV Millennial Awards (Latin America)
2018: K-Pop Revolution (Won) Fandom of the Year
(Won)

MTV Millennial Awards (Brazil)
2018: K-Pop Explosion (Won) Fandom of the Year
(Won)

*MTV Video Music A*wards (Japan)
2018: Best Group Video (Fake Love) Won

Teen Choice Awards
2017: Choice International Artist (Won)
2018: Choice International Artist (Won) Choice
Fandom Award (Won)

The Asian Awards
2018: Outstanding Achievement in Music (Won)

The Hall of Stars Awards
2018: Best Fandom (Spain) (Won)
Best Fandom Worldwide (Won)

YinYueTai V Chart Awards
2014: Rookie Award (Won)
2017: Best Stage Performance Award (Won)

Sources

Magazines

Billboard, Forbes, Elle, Cuvism, Time, BTS Japan Fan, Grazia Korea, Ize, K Plus, Onni, Rolling Stone, Fuse, Hollywood Reporter, Variety

Newspapers

K-Pop Herald, Orange County Register, New York Times, Bucks County Courier Times, Burlington County Times

Websites

A Side.com, Vox.com, BTS Live.com, Fandom.com, CNBC.com, Soompi.com, Affinity.com, Celebmix.com, Sports Seoul.com, BTS.com, Metro Uk.com, BTS Melon Showcase.com, K Style.com, Kulturescene.com, Naverstarcast.com, Kpopstarz.com, Amino.com, BTS Diary.com, My Metro.com, Quora.com, Koreaboo.com, Korea Portal.com, Kpopism.com, Newseveryday.com, Straits Times.com, Digital Music News.com, E News.com, Hollywood Life.com, Popasia.com. X Ports News.com, BTSTrans.com

Television

The Ellen DeGeneres Show, Same Bed Different Dreams, Koogle TV, Naver TV, CNN, Entertainment Tonight, NBCS5

Miscellaneous

Burn the Stage (You Tube Series), Australian press conference, Various media press, conferences, *MSO* public relations interview, *Bangtan's Subs Channel*, *Big Hit Entertainment* press statements. *The Grammy Museum* interview

About the Author

New York Times bestselling author Marc Shapiro has written more than 60 nonfiction celebrity biographies, more than two-dozen comic books, numerous short stories and poetry, and three short form screenplays. He is also a veteran freelance entertainment journalist.

His young adult book *JK Rowling: The Wizard Behind Harry Potter* was on *The New York Times* bestseller list for four straight weeks. His fact-based book *Total Titanic* was also on *The Los Angeles Times* bestseller list for four weeks. *Justin Bieber: The Fever* was on the nationwide Canadian bestseller list for several weeks.

Shapiro has written books on such personalities as Shonda Rhimes, George Harrison, Carlos Santana, Annette Funicello, Lorde, Lindsay Johan, E.L. James, Jamie Dornan, Dakota Johnson, Adele and countless others. He also co-authored the autobiography of mixed martial arts fighter Tito Ortiz, *This Is Gonna Hurt: The Life of a Mixed Martial Arts Champion*.

He is currently working on a biography of the rock group Greta Van Fleet as well as updating his biographies of Gillian Anderson and Lucy Lawless for Riverdale Avenue Books.

Other Riverdale Avenue Books Titles by Marc Shapiro

Lorde: Your Heroine, How This Young Feminist Broke the Rules and Succeeded

Legally Bieber: Justin Bieber at 18

You're Gonna Make It After All: The Life, Times and Influence of Mary Tyler Moore

Hey Joe: The Unauthorized Biography of a Rock Classic

Trump This! The Life and Times of Donald Trump, An Unauthorized Biography

The Secret Life of EL James

The Real Steele: The Unauthorized Biography of Dakota Johnson

Inside Grey's Anatomy: The Unauthorized Biography of Jamie Dornan

Annette Funicello: America's Sweetheart

Game: The Resurrection of Tim Tebow

Lindsay Lohan: Fully Loaded, From Disney to Disaster

We Love Jenni: An Unauthorized Biography

Who Is Katie Holmes? An Unauthorized Biography

Norman Reedus: True Tales of The Waking Dead's Zombie Hunter, An Unauthorized Biography

Welcome to Shondaland: An Unauthorized Biography of Shonda Rhimes

Renaissance man: The Lin Manuel Story

John McCain: View from the Hill